# THE FIG

_Hayden Childs_ (signature)

# LEAVES

## End Time Prophecies

William Hayden Childs, MD, MBA

Book Layout ©2017 BookDesignTemplates.com

Ordering Information: figleavesministry.gmail

Quantity sales. Special discounts are available on quantity purchases by corporations, associations, and others. For details, contact the author at the address above.

Bible quotations are primarily from NIV, and NASB

"Scripture taken from the HOLY BIBLE, NEW INTERNATIONAL VERSION. ® Copyright © 1973, 1978, 1984 International Bible Society. Used by permission of Zondervan Bible Publishers."

"Scripture taken from the NEW AMERICAN STANDARD BIBLE , Copyright © 1960, 1962, 1963, 1968, 1971, 1972, 1973, 1975, 1977, 1995 by The Lockman Foundation. Used by permission."

The Fig Leaves/William Hayden Childs —1st ed.

Cover Design by Ryan Gausman

Images by Kendal James & Ricard Gomez Angel--Unsplash

ISBN 978-1-63183-411-0

# Contents

*I would like to thank all of the people who have encouraged me in the writing and publishing of this book, and helped in the editing of the text:*
*Special thanks to Charles Myers, Loretta Goetting, my niece, Julia Gibbs, and my wife, Jule Childs*

*"Now learn a lesson from the fig tree.  When her branch is tender and the leaves begin to sprout, you know that summer is almost here.  Just so, when you see all these things beginning to happen, you can know that My return is near, even at the doors."*

–Matthew 24:32-33

# Introduction

This book is the outcome of a prophecy study I assisted our pastor in teaching at our church around 2007. I am not a theologian and do not have a degree in Biblical studies. I have read the prophetic words of the Bible and taught and written what the Holy Spirit has put in my heart and mind. God has spoken to mankind in different modalities: directly, through angels, through visions and dreams, through prophets, and through His written (revealed) Word. I am not a prophet. I have never been given direct prophetic instructions from God. I have only studied and tried to discern the Truth in His Word. There are obviously many schools of thought that diverge over whether interpretations of prophetic Scripture should be understood to be literal or figurative. I do state without apology that the prophecies as I read them are clearly literal in their application to future events. In this matter, I can only hope to be a vessel for the Lord.

Having declared for the literal interpretations, one is obliged to note that there is obviously much figurative imagery used symbolically in these prophecies. Does Satan actually look like a red dragon with seven heads and ten horns as described in Revelation 12:3?[1] And does the believing remnant of Israel actually use eagles' wings to fly to safety as in Revelation 12:14?[2] Does our Lord actually have a sword protruding from His mouth upon His return as stated in

---

[1] The Bible, God through many authors: *"Then another sign appeared in heaven: an enormous red dragon with seven heads and ten horns and seven crowns on its heads."* Revelation 12:3.

[2] The Bible, God through many authors: *"The woman was given the two wings of a great eagle, so that she might fly to the place prepared for her in the wilderness ..."* Revelation 12:14a

1

Revelation 19:15?[3] In my opinion, probably "no" to all of these figurative images; but even though they are symbolic, they all do have a meaning relative to the things of this world.

Satan's work in the Tribulation may be done by a union of seven nations, or alliances, with ten leaders. The remnant of Israel will in some way be able to fly to safety during the Tribulation. And our Lord will destroy His enemies with His voice as He quotes the ancient Scriptures. The Holy Spirit gave the prophets visions that included symbols that were strange and perhaps unintelligible for the man of that era, but laden with meaning for the people closer to the events as they occur. How would the apostle John know what he was seeing, if he saw an airplane in a vision? The only things that flew in his day were birds, and one of the largest birds he would have known was the eagle. The Holy Spirit would probably not show John a vision of an airplane since he would not know how to even describe it in his day. But he may have been shown a vision of large wings carrying the remnant to safety Revelation 12:14.

Since the earliest years of Christianity, men have suggested figurative meanings for the difficult symbolic language of much of God's Word. These figurative interpretations have been the mainstream thought for much of the Church for many centuries now. No one has yet explained why the simple literal meanings are not appropriate.

Another tremendous force working on the modern reader is "secular" Science. When the sophisticated and highly educated scientist talks about the "natural" beginnings of the universe, and explains how it all just came about without God, this slowly infuses into the mindset of the student. This ideology can permeate the mindset and

---

[3] The Bible, God through many authors; "*Coming out of his mouth is a sharp sword with which to strike down the nations...*" Revelation 19:15a.

worldview of those educated in that manner to the extent that literal interpretation of the Bible seems foolish.

I was educated as a scientist, and considered myself a part of the scientific community until the 1990s, when many of the "leading" scientists began to assault religion en masse. Many scientists have locked arms and declared unequivocally that there is no God, and that the universe and nature all have a "rational" beginning and evolution. (Interestingly, no one in the Science camp can explain how life began on earth.) Anyone who does not conform to the "naturalistic" view is usually excluded from serious scientific discourse. In a major twist of irony, scientists have invented a new religion. Its god is "Naturalistic Science," and its high priests will excommunicate anyone who does not conform to its dogma. I have always believed that true science is man's attempt to retro-engineer God's creation. Also, the scientific method requires questioning everything that we think we know. When that questioning is squelched, the resulting methodology is no longer scientific, but rather becomes dogmatic.

Ironically, it is the science of archaeology that is continuing to uncover more and more evidence that supports the stories of the Bible, and is therefore confirming its truth.

God's Word was written under the direction of the Holy Spirit and has layers of meanings. A "novice" Christian who is reading the Scriptures for the first time will continue to find deeper meanings in the same Scriptures as his or her faith matures. The psalmist says, *"Deep calls to deep..."* Psalms 42:7, and again, *"The unfolding of Your words give light; it gives understanding to the simple."* Psalms 119:130. The closer one gets to God, the deeper and more profound meanings will be drawn from His Word.

This is especially true of the rich symbolism given to His prophets. Often they reveal an occurrence that will soon follow.  But they also may point to events in the distant and unfathomable (for the prophet) future.  Ezekiel, an exile in Babylon in the 6th century B.C., had a vision of the Israelites coming back into the Holy Land and being reformed as a nation.  This vision is revealed in Ezekiel 37:1-28.  This remarkable event occurred within 100 years of his vision, as the new King of Persia released the remnant survivors of the Captivity to return and rebuild Jerusalem.  But it occurred again in 1948, when the modern nation of Israel was proclaimed a new nation.

Scripture helps reveal Scripture.  Isaiah, a prophet over a hundred years before Ezekiel, wrote
*"Now in that day the remnant of Israel...will return, the remnant of Jacob, will return to the mighty God."* Isaiah 10:20-21.
Isaiah also revealed, *"Then it will happen on that day that the Lord will **again recover the second time** with His hand the remnant of His people, who will remain, from Assyria, Egypt, Pathros, Cush, Elam, Shinar, Hamath, and from the islands of the sea."* Isaiah 12:11.
Ezekiel was shown the rebuilding of Israel, and Isaiah was shown that that event would not happen just once, but twice (537 B.C. and 1948 A.D.)

As you read the Scriptures that contain the prophecies, pray for illumination by the Holy Spirit, the One who first infused these oracles into the prophets.  If the meanings revealed to you are different from those of other Christian brothers or sisters, discuss it with them.  *"Iron sharpens iron, so one person sharpens another"* Proverbs 27:17.  Beware of people who are trying to promote themselves instead of giving credit and glory to God.  The Apostle Paul said that prophecy is to edify the Church.  Any other purpose runs counter to God's Word.

Several interpretative versions of the Bible are quoted in this book. The most quoted version is the NIV, but also the NASB.

This book is divided into two main sections. Section 1 explores the prophecies about the End Times, and exposition of those prophecies. Section 2 is a discussion of the events leading up to the seven-year Tribulation, the events during the Tribulation, and the events following the Tribulation.

.

# SECTION I

## END TIMES
## PROPHECIES

# CHAPTER 1

# The Fig Leaves

The end of the world as we know it has both fascinated the minds of some and struck fear in the hearts of others for centuries. In the 1950s many movies were made that played on the new Atomic Age narrative as producing scenarios that could lead to the end of the world. As a boy, I remember the fear of the giant ants in the movie, "Them," that threatened to take over the world and destroy all mankind. Another movie, "The Incredible Shrinking Man," told the story of a man exposed to a radioactive fog and subsequently began to shrink. He became smaller and smaller, and had to fight with small animals and then a spider that tried to kill him. These battles were very terrifying, and then in the end of the movie, he shrank away to nothing. The overarching fear of that era was the obliteration of the world by a nuclear war. The movie, "The Day the World Stood Still," had a character from outer space who threatened to destroy the earth if its inhabitants did not destroy their nuclear weapons. He stated that the other inhabitants of the universe would not tolerate the possible effects of such large explosions.

More recently, some secular TV series have shown what the world would supposedly look like after humans have become extinct. Movies have been made about major catastrophes occurring that destroy most if not all of humankind, and the post-apocalyptic world that remains. People are watching the movements of stars and planets, looking for signs that might indicate whether the end of everything has come upon us. The human angst in the early twenty-first century revolves around whether the earth will be able to continue to support the ever-increasing population of humans. How will the human race survive in the future?

Even Christians are feeling an urgency that time is running out for this age. We find ourselves asking, what is actually happening now? Should we start worrying about the End of the World? Does the Bible tell us what is coming? Do we have any instructions about how we should respond?

In Christian theology, the end of this world occurs at the time of the Second Coming of Jesus. This book is meant to help those who "have eyes" and those who "have ears" to "see" and to "hear," and to be able to discern the signs of the times.

The parable of the fig tree was used by Jesus to answer his disciples' question about when He would return, and what signs would let them know that He would soon come. When all the trees are beginning to sprout their new leaves in the springtime, the fig tree is one of the last to put out its leaves, usually just before summer. Jesus told His disciples what signs to look for, and when they would see them, they would know that His return was imminent. When we see these signs happening, and recognize that they are the signs that God has given us, we can know that God is continuing to work in this world. He indeed has a timeline that stretches from His creation of this world to its very end! The signs, or "Fig Leaves" described here let us know that He is bringing His world into the last part of that timeline—the End Times.

The signs given to us through biblical prophecy are beginning to show up all around us now. If we know the

Scriptures, we should be able to recognize them as they occur. Jesus, in using the parable of the fig tree, expects us to use our discernment to understand what is happening in the world today, and what that may mean regarding our future. For almost two thousand years now people have tried to perceive if they were living in the End Times. The cartoon character dressed as a bearded prophet in a robe, carrying a sign saying, "The End Is Near" has been a running joke for many years because the Christian end times scenario has always been disconcerting--if not downright scary--for non-Christians.

It can be very frightening for Christians also. In the early 1970s, I read one of the first best-selling books portraying a scenario of the End Times as described by Biblical prophecy.[4] After reading the book, even though I considered myself a "good" Christian, I was frightened and upset. I had recently married and had a small child, and I was building my career, and now the world was going to end?

Like so many other Christians, I had not fully submitted my life to the Lord. I still had my own plans for my life and the thought of everything ending was scary. Unfortunately, I had focused so much on the destruction scenario in the book that I missed the little explanation at the end that explained how well everything would turn out. We have a Father who will save and indeed rescue His children. Today, many people, Christians and non-Christians alike, are concerned about world events and what those events mean for their futures.

Worrying about current world events and their consequences keep many people anxious and sleepless. Will we have a nuclear holocaust that destroys all of mankind? Will our country's morality and social mores continue to worsen to the point that we will not be safe in our homes? Are

---

[4] The Late Great Planet Earth, Hal Lindsey, Zondervan Publishing House, 1970

our children safe in school? How can our economy continue to function in the face of such volatile oil prices? How can we overcome or even withstand the Islamic terrorists who want to destroy us? These questions plus the everyday pressures and problems of our individual lives cause many nights of lost sleep for people all over the world.

Jesus, however, taught us that we need not worry because God is in control and will watch over us

*"So do not worry about tomorrow; for tomorrow will worry about itself. Each day has enough trouble of its own."* <u>Matthew 6:34</u>

However, we often do not take His word completely to heart. We continue to worry about world events and what that might mean for us and our families. The American government actually employs people who spend all of their time studying various countries that might threaten the U.S. in the future. They try to forecast possible scenarios in which these countries would actively cause harm to the U.S. and/or to its citizens. They use political and economic parameters in their projections. They would have a clearer view of world events if they would use Biblical prophecy to help their forecasts.

Studying the words of Jesus and the prophets to discover and understand the signs, or "fig leaves," which would indicate the onset of the End Times, could lead to various differing scenarios derived from the same prophecies. Even if we are able to discern the individual "fig leaves," we still do not really know in what order they may occur. Other interpretations may put different emphasis on certain prophecies, and may discern different sequences for the signs.

As God's prophecies--the fig leaves--are revealed to us, we can place them in the perspective of God's plan for this world, and continue to praise God without worrying so much about what will happen in the next hundred years. We know how things will come out, because we have read His Word, the Bible. As His prophecies unfold, we can indeed be assured that this is God's world.

# CHAPTER 2

# What Is Prophecy?

What do we mean when we use the word "prophecy?" The most common use in our culture today is a foretelling of future events. The Greek word *Propheteia* signifies the "speaking forth of the mind and counsel of God" according to Vine's Dictionary of Old and New Testament Words.[5] Vine's Dictionary explains that while "much of O.T. prophecy was purely predictive, prophecy is not necessarily, nor even primarily, fore-telling. It is the declaration of that which cannot be known by natural means...it is the forth-telling of the will of God, whether with reference to the past, the present, or the future." Prophecy has been described as a "mode of special revelation ... (whereby) God reasserted Himself as the ultimate interpreter of truth."[6] When the Apostle Paul discusses prophecy in the 14th chapter of 1 Corinthians, he is not concerned about the revelation of the future but rather the revelation of the mind of God.

---

[5] Vine's Expository Dictionary of Old and New Testament Words, ed. F.F. Bruce, Fleming H. Revell Co., 1981. p. 221.

[6] Dictionary of Theological Terms, Alan Cairns, Ambassador-Emerald International, 2002. p.347.

*"Follow the way of love and eagerly desire gifts of the Spirit, especially prophecy ... But the one who prophesies speaks to people for their strengthening, encouraging and comfort. Anyone who speaks in a tongue edifies themselves, but the one who prophesies edifies the church."* <u>1 Corinthians 14: 1,3,4</u>

While "prophecy" means much more than just revealing the future, we will, in this book, look at its more restricted meaning of foretelling the future.

John Walvoord, considered by many as one of the foremost experts on prophecy, stated that one-fourth of all of the verses of the Bible are concerned with foretelling the future.[7] He postulated that God obviously wanted us to have some indication of what His plans and purposes were for the human race and universe as a whole. He further stated that approximately half of the prophecies have already been fulfilled. Certainly the Bible has put forth predictions that have already come true.

Two remarkable prophecies are said to have had a significant impact on the course of history for the Jewish people according to Josephus, a Jewish historian who lived in the 1st century A.D.(C.E.). The first amazing prophecy was the actual naming of the Persian king, Cyrus, by Isaiah some 100 years before his (Cyrus's) birth.

*"I am the **LORD** who says of Cyrus, 'He is my shepherd and will accomplish all that I please.'... "This is what the **LORD** says to his anointed, to Cyrus, whose right hand I take hold of to subdue nations before him and to strip kings of their armor, to open doors before him so that gates will not be shut: I will go before you and will level the mountains; I will break down gates of bronze and cut through bars of iron.*
*I will give you hidden treasures, riches stored in secret*

---

[7] <u>Every Prophecy of the Bible</u>, John F. Walvoord, David C. Cook, 1999. p. 10.

*places, so that you may know that I am the LORD, the God of Israel, who summons you by name. For the sake of Jacob my servant, of Israel my chosen, I summon you by name and bestow on you a title of honor, though you do not acknowledge me.*

*I am the LORD, and there is no other; apart from me there is no God. I will strengthen you, though you have not acknowledged me,..."* Isaiah 44:28, 45:1-5

Josephus wrote that "he (God) stirred up the mind of Cyrus, and made him write this throughout all Asia:--'Thus saith Cyrus the King:--Since God Almighty hath appointed me to be king of the habitable earth, I believe that he is that God which the nation of the Israelites worship; for indeed he foretold my name by the prophets; and that I should build him a house at Jerusalem, in the country of Judea.' This was known to Cyrus by his reading the book which Isaiah left behind him of his prophecies; for this prophet said that God had spoken thus to him in a secret vision:--'My will is, that Cyrus, whom I have appointed to be king over many and great nations, send back my people to their own land, and build my temple.' This was foretold by Isaiah one hundred and forty years before the temple was demolished. Accordingly, when Cyrus read this, and admired the divine power, an earnest desire and ambition seized upon him to fulfill what was so written."[8]

Thus, according to Josephus, the prophecies of Isaiah were instrumental in the return of the Jews to Jerusalem after their captivity.

Jeremiah was a prophet in Jerusalem during the time it was destroyed by the Babylonians. It was his prophecies to the exiles in Babylon when they were first carried there that stirred up Daniel and others to ask Cyrus and other rulers to let them return to Jerusalem.

---

[8] The Antiquities of the Jews, Book 11, Chap. 1, Flavius Josephus, Hendrickson Publishers, Inc., 1987

*"This is what the LORD says: "When seventy years are completed for Babylon, I will come to you and fulfill my good promise to bring you back to this place."* <u>Jeremiah 29:10</u>

Daniel, the prophet who served the kings of Babylon and Media-Persia during the exile, realized that the seventy years of exile were coming to an end.

*"In the first year of Darius son of Xerxes (a Mede by descent), who was made ruler over the Babylonian kingdom— in the first year of his reign, I, Daniel, understood from the Scriptures, according to the word of the LORD given to Jeremiah the prophet, that the desolation of Jerusalem would last seventy years."* <u>Daniel 9:1-2</u>

Daniel's prayer to God for the restoration of Jerusalem and Israel is recorded in Daniel 9:3-19.[9] Ezra also recounts the

---

[9] <u>The Bible</u>, God through many authors; *"So I turned to the Lord God and pleaded with him in prayer and petition, in fasting, and in sackcloth and ashes. I prayed to the LORD my God and confessed: "Lord, the great and awesome God, who keeps his covenant of love with those who love him and keep his commandments, we have sinned and done wrong. We have been wicked and have rebelled; we have turned away from your commands and laws. We have not listened to your servants the prophets, who spoke in your name to our kings, our princes and our ancestors, and to all the people of the land. "Lord, you are righteous, but this day we are covered with shame—the people of Judah and the inhabitants of Jerusalem and all Israel, both near and far, in all the countries where you have scattered us because of our unfaithfulness to you. We and our kings, our princes and our ancestors are covered with shame, LORD, because we have sinned against you. The Lord our God is merciful and forgiving, even though we have rebelled against him; we have not obeyed the LORD our God or kept the laws he gave us through his servants the prophets. All Israel has transgressed your law and turned away, refusing to obey you. Therefore the curses and sworn judgments written in the Law of Moses, the servant of God, have been poured out on us, because we have sinned against you. You have fulfilled the words spoken against us and against our rulers by bringing on us great disaster. Under the whole heaven nothing has ever been done like what has been done to Jerusalem. Just as it is written in the Law of Moses, all this disaster has come on us, yet we have not sought the favor of the LORD our God by turning from our sins and giving attention to your truth. The LORD did not hesitate to bring the disaster on us, for the LORD our God is righteous in everything he does; yet we have not obeyed him. Now, Lord our God, who brought your people out of Egypt with a mighty hand and who made for yourself a name that endures to this day, we have sinned, we have done wrong. Lord, in keeping with all your righteous acts, turn away your anger and your wrath from Jerusalem, your city, your holy hill. Our sins and the iniquities of our ancestors have made Jerusalem and your people an object of scorn to all those around us. Now, our God, hear the prayers and petitions of your servant. For your sake, Lord, look with favor on your desolate sanctuary. Give ear, our God, and hear; open your eyes and see the desolation of the city that bears your Name. We do not make requests of you because we are righteous, but because of your great mercy. Lord, listen! Lord, forgive! Lord, hear*

instigation of the Jewish restoration of Jerusalem in the beginning of his book—and also in the final verses of 2 Chronicles, alluded to by Josephus in previous pages:

*"In the first year of Cyrus king of Persia, in order to fulfill the word of the LORD spoken by Jeremiah, the LORD moved the heart of Cyrus king of Persia to make a proclamation throughout his realm and also to put it in writing:*
*"This is what Cyrus king of Persia says: 'The LORD, the God of heaven, has given me all the kingdoms of the earth and he has appointed me to build a temple for him at Jerusalem in Judah.'"* Ezra 1:1-2

This great prophecy was revealed by God to His people, and then God arranged and orchestrated its fulfillment. In the same way, we can believe and expect all of God's prophecies will be fulfilled. This world remains in God's hands, and all of His Words will be fulfilled.

The second great fulfillment of ancient prophecy occurred about a hundred years after the rebuilding of Jerusalem and the temple. Alexander the Great of Macedonia and conqueror of all of Greece, was in the process of conquering the entire known world of his era, including the Eastern Mediterranean area. After defeating the Persian army at the battle of Issus in 333 B.C., near the current border of Turkey and Syria, Alexander quickly moved down the Mediterranean shore to the city of Tyre, which is now in Lebanon. The battle of Tyre required seven months of siege, which infuriated Alexander, who then subjected the surviving Tyrians to the harsh fate of slavery. After finally destroying Tyre, he then marched south toward Egypt and conquered the city of Gaza, southwest of Jerusalem.

Having secured the eastern Mediterranean coast, he turned his army inland and marched toward Jerusalem

---

*and act! For your sake, my God, do not delay, because your city and your people bear your Name."* Daniel 9:3-19 intending to destroy it as noted by Josephus. Daniel, the prophet, had seen the king of Greece in one of his visions sometime around 553-540 B.C. and recorded it as follows:

*"While I was observing, behold, a male goat was coming from the west over the surface of the whole earth without touching the ground; and the goat had a conspicuous horn between his eyes.*

*He came up to the ram that had the two horns, which I had seen standing in front of the canal, and rushed at him in his mighty wrath. I saw him come beside the ram, and he was enraged at him;*

*and he struck the ram and shattered his two horns, and the ram had no strength to withstand him.*

*So he hurled him to the ground and trampled on him, and there was none to rescue the ram from his power."* Daniel 8:5-7

Then the angel Gabriel was given orders to explain this to Daniel.

*"The two-horned ram that you saw represents the kings of Media and Persia. The shaggy goat is the king of Greece, and the large horn between its eyes is the first king."* Daniel 8:20-21

This prophecy was given to Daniel over two hundred years before Alexander began his conquests!

The Jewish historian, Josephus, tells us that Alexander, while besieging Tyre, sent a letter to the Jewish high priest, asking for troops and provisions;

"...but the high priest answered the messengers, that he had given his oath to Darius not to bear arms against him and he said that he would not transgress this while Darius was in the land of the living. Upon hearing this answer, Alexander was very angry; and ...he threatened that he would make an expedition against the Jewish high priest, and through him teach all men to whom they must keep their oaths. ...Now Alexander, when he had taken Gaza, made haste to go up to

Jerusalem; and Jaddua the high priest, when he heard that, was in an agony, and under terror, as not knowing how he should meet the Macedonians, since the king was displeased at his foregoing disobedience. ...whereupon God warned him in a dream...that he should take courage, and adorn the city, and open the gates; that the rest appear in white garments, but that he and the priests should meet the king in the habits proper to their order, without the dread of any ill consequences, which the providence of God would prevent. ...And when he (Jaddua) understood that he (Alexander) was not far from the city, he went out in procession, with the priests and the multitude of the citizens. The procession was venerable, and the manner of it different from that of other nations. ...for Alexander, when he saw the multitude at a distance, in white garments, while the priests stood clothed with fine linen, and the high priest in purple and scarlet clothing, with his miter on his head having the golden plate on which the name of God was engraved, he approached by himself, and adored that name, and first saluted the high priest. The Jews also did all together, with one voice, salute Alexander." When Alexander's general, Parmenio, approached the great leader and asked him why he had honored the high priest instead of trampling him down, Alexander replied, "I did not adore him, but that God who hath honored him with that high priesthood; for I saw this very person in a dream, in this very habit, when I was at Dios, in Macedonia, who, when I was considering with myself how I might obtain the dominion of Asia, exhorted me to make no delay, but boldly pass over the sea thither, for that he would conduct my army, and would give me the dominion over the Persians" "...and when he went up into the temple, he offered sacrifice to God, according to the high priest's direction, and magnificently treated both the high priest and the priests. And when the book of Daniel was showed him, wherein Daniel declared that one of the Greeks should destroy the empire of the Persians, he supposed that himself was the person intended; and as he was glad, he ...granted...that they (the Jews) might enjoy the laws of the forefathers."[10]

Because of God's prophecy to Daniel, and His giving dreams to both Alexander and the High Priest, Jerusalem was saved from Alexander's ire, and the Jews were given special privileges to worship God wherever they might be in Alexander's kingdom.

Not everyone accepts that these examples of prophecies are true. Many biblical scholars since the late 1800s have been educated in a philosophy of biblical formation called "rationalistic higher criticism". Higher criticism is the "scholarly investigation of the date, authorship, place, and circumstances of composition of the books of the Bible, together with a study of their purpose and nature...While conservative scholars reverently base their investigations on an honest recognition of the inspiration, infallibility, and authority of the Bible, rationalistic higher critics have always reduced it to merely a human level—even when the passage of time and patient investigation has subsequently proved the fallacy of their notions."[11]

These liberal scholars who follow the higher critical philosophies of Wellhausen[12] (Documentary Hypothesis) and Bultmann[13] (Form Criticism) have maintained that any Biblical prediction that has already been fulfilled would actually have been written after the event, therefore supposedly accounting for the accuracy of these predictions. These scholars started with the premise that the historical events set forth in the Bible were myths, and should be discarded in studying

[10] The Antiquities of the Jews, Book 11, Chap. 8, Flavius Josephus, Hendrickson Publishers, Inc. 1987

[11] Dictionary of Theological Terms, Alan Cairns, ibid, p. 118.

[12] Die Composition des Hexateuchs, Julius Wellhausen, Berlin, 1899

[13] Form Criticism, "The Study of the Synoptic Gospels," Rudolf Bultmann, Ed. By F. C. Grant, Willett, Clark and Co., 1934

Scripture.[14] This failed scholastic school of thought has been refuted time and again by further archeological and historical findings,[15] and yet is so embedded in today's religious educational institutions, that many or perhaps, almost all seminary students are taught this now.

This is not meant to cast doubt on all textual criticism. This methodology of scrupulous study of ancient texts has yielded transmission errors (mistakes in copying and interpretation) and added to our understanding of scripture over the centuries. But any criticism that begins with the premise that the original manuscripts (known as "autographs" by biblical scholars) were the results of merely the cultural and ideological concepts of that age and not inspired by God would automatically refute any prophecy contained in those manuscripts as concepts of man and not of God. Those who believe in the prophetic foretelling of future events, hold firmly to the premise of the inerrancy of the original manuscripts in revealing God's mind to us. God wanted to give us a view of future events, revealing them to many of the authors of the books in the Bible.

In no other religion are future events revealed as in the Bible. The great take-away from this is that the fulfillment of these prophecies show without a doubt that there is Truth in the Bible! Imagine if the Bible had been lost to mankind for two thousand years, and just recently re-discovered. People would be amazed and awed to find a book that so correctly predicted so many world events! And yet today, due to the intrusive Humanism in our society, this book is described by many as a collection of old superstitions. The great underlying Truth behind these prophecies is that God is real, and He has given us proof by telling us about future events.

---

[14] Dictionary of Theological Terms, Alan Cairns, ibid, p.294.
[15] The New Evidence That Demands a Verdict, Josh McDowell, Thomas Nelson Publishers, 1999:Chap. 13, "Archaeology and Biblical Criticism"

Joel Rosenberg, in his book, *Epicenter*, makes the following statement: "While it is fashionable in our times to analyze world events merely by looking through the lenses of politics and economics, it is also a serious mistake, for it prevents one from being able to see in three dimensions. To truly understand the significance of global events and trends, one must analyze them through a third lens as well: the lens of Scripture."[16] He credits the success of his novels in predicting events in the Middle East to this principle he calls the "Third Lens". Indeed, many of the prophecies of Ezekiel and Jesus Himself are appearing before us now, and with discernment one can see that these are the first of the "fig leaves."

Actual dates for the "fig leaves" are not usually given to us by prophecy. Those who have dared to predict an actual date of any particular event usually have been wrong. However, by using the Parable of the Fig Tree that Jesus told us, we can see what has already happened and try to determine what events are to come. Certainly more signs have occurred in our time than during any other generation before us. When the disciples of Jesus asked when and where all of his prophesies regarding the End Times would come, He said to them,

*"Where there is a dead body, there the vultures will gather."* Luke 17:37

This was a familiar proverb in His time that essentially pointed out that one vulture circling overhead does not mean much, but when there is a gathering of vultures, there is a dead carcass around somewhere.[17] Likewise, when one sign of the End Times occurs, it may not be very significant, but when many signs begin to occur, people should be ready for the End

---

[16] Epicenter, Joel Rosenberg, Tyndale House Publishers, Inc., 2006, p.47
[17] Life Application Bible, Zondervan Corporation, 2000, textual note for Luke 17:37

Times. As we see more and more "fig leaves" on the tree, we begin to understand the times.

Where do the United States and other Western countries fall in Biblical prophecy? The U.S. is not mentioned as a major "player" in Biblical prophecy. Some European countries could be involved in the reformation of the new Roman Empire. But the focus of the world will move to Israel as we move further into the "End Times." The United States has been the major protector of Israel since its founding in 1948. As we will see through Ezekiel's prophecies, a time is coming when Israel will be attacked by a large army led by Russians and Iranians. The U.S. will probably do no more than attempt to negotiate with Russia and Iran, but will not help Israel. Actually, no other country in the world will ally with Israel and offer it protection. God—and only God—will protect Israel with His mighty power, demonstrating His great love for Israel and His chosen people.

This prophecy indicates that the U.S. will no longer be a superpower. The U.S. economy will no longer be the premier economy in the world. The American dollar will not be the predominant currency of the world. In recent times, we have seen other countries promoting other currencies to replace the dollar. With the faltering U.S. economy and increasing national debt, foreseeing the U.S.'s slide from the "superpower" position it has held since World War II is not difficult. In the near future, when Israel is threatened, the U.S. will have a president and a Congress who will want to negotiate at the most critical of times. Soon afterwards, the Anti-Christ and the One World Government will rise out of the chaos and become the dominant world power.

But as we keep saying, regardless of the fate of any particular country, this is God's world, and while the future has some very big bumps, the final outcome is wonderful.

The prophet Isaiah was given the following words from God:

*"Remember this, keep it in mind, take it to heart, you rebels. Remember the former things, those of long ago; I am God, and there is no other; I am God, and there is none like me. I make known the end from the beginning, from ancient times, what is still to come. I say, 'My purpose will stand, and I will do all that I please.'"* Isaiah 46:8-10

# CHAPTER 3

# Eschatology

Eschatology refers to the study of "end times". In most cases, eschatology is tied to religious beliefs. For humanists, secularists and followers of "Scientism", the future is very insecure and frightening because of all the uncertain possibilities. Those who believe that Science is the only hope for the future also seem to believe that mankind will either become extinct in the future, or will migrate to other planets in the universe (think "Star Trek"). This then is their "eschatology." Humanists have always dreamed of "Utopia" on earth. Their view of the future is a society where all people are free and can help make the world a better place to live. Implicit in this eschatology is the concept that all peoples on the earth can come together to form a united culture and society. At least, this has been the idea of the future up until recently.

When Darwin published his book, *The Origin of the Species*, in 1859, and when Karl Marx's trilogy, *Das Kapital*, was published a few years later, Western mankind lived in an age of optimism. The Zeitgeist, or Spirit of the Age as C.S. Lewis alluded to it, was a Hegelian concept of the ever-improvement of mankind until that future utopian society was built. Darwin envisioned the evolution of mankind to become more perfect intellectually and physically. Marx envisioned the evolution of society to become more perfect in dealing with the problems of poverty and oppression.

However, the Spirit of the Age has changed; that change occurring sometime during the 1970s-1980s. Some historians think that the destruction of the Berlin Wall, with its signaling the end of the Cold War was the turning point. With the threat of nuclear war reduced, men could turn their angst to other areas. More likely, it began to change after the 1960s with its cultural wars and shifting mores. Also, the Club of Rome was established in 1968, and in the 1970s published several books that challenged traditional thinking[18].

One of their statements noted that *"The common enemy of humanity is man. In searching for a new enemy to unite us, we came up with the idea that pollution, the threat of global warming, water shortages, famine and the like would fit the bill. All of these dangers are caused by human intervention, and it is only through changed attitudes and behavior that they can be overcome. **The real enemy then, is humanity itself.**"* (Aurelio Peccei, founding member of the Club of Rome)[19]

From out of the wonderful, well-meaning Conservation Movement emerged a darker and more sinister concept. No longer is humanity thought of from the Christian view as the children of God caring for this earth of ours. Now mankind, under the new Spirit of the Age, is seen as an infestation on the planet—a species among other species without special uniqueness—that is gradually destroying the planet. In 1993, the United Nations published a conceptual paper that outlined how our species might survive on earth in the future. Called

---

[18] The Limits of Growth(1972), Mankind at the Turning Point(1975), Reshaping the International Order(1976), and Goals for Mankind(1977)
[19] "Aurelio Peccei." AZQuotes.com. Wind and Fly LTD, 2018. 30 July 2018. https://www.azquotes.com/author/46173-Aurelio_Peccei

Agenda 21, this paper proposed that areas of the world would be off-limits to humans to maintain a sustainable environment, and also, the population of the world would have to be reduced by some undetermined means.

This humanist concept will probably be used by those individuals who want to increase their own power and wealth in the future, and will push for a World Government and a world currency. Unfortunately, humankind at its very core would have to undergo a dramatic change to bring about a utopian world. The humanist societies that the world has had to endure during the twentieth century have not worked out very well. Communist Russia brought about the abominations and oppressions of Stalin, and Nazi Germany birthed the horrors of the Holocaust. Humanists continue to indoctrinate our culture with socialist ideas to "further mankind", in spite of the previous failures of the humanist societies.

*The Humanist Manifesto II* (1973) puts forth seventeen principles regarding humankind. The first principle states that "...traditional dogmatic or authoritarian religions that place revelation, God, ritual, or creed above human needs and experience do a disservice to the human species. ...We find insufficient evidence for belief in the existence of a supernatural; ...No deity will save us; we must save ourselves."

The second principle states that "...science affirms that the human species is an emergence from natural evolutionary forces...There is no credible evidence that life survives the death of the body."

In its closing paragraphs, the Manifesto states, "the world cannot wait for a reconciliation of competing political or economic systems to solve its problems... commitment to all humankind is the highest commitment of which we are capable; it transcends the narrow allegiances of church, state, party, class, or race in moving toward a wider vision of human potentiality."[20]

The beliefs set forth in this manifesto have become the underpinnings of the new American and European society. No longer do the people of the Western countries base cultural and moral values on Judeo-Christian principles. The U.S. legal system is moving into the hands of judges who have bought into the corrupted version of the First Amendment that dictates that religion shall not be allowed in the public square.

In contrast, the Christian view is that we live in a fallen world, and that human efforts alone will never result in a utopian society. There will always be a Lenin or Hitler around to highjack any movement that attempts to build a society that would supposedly improve mankind's condition through governmental efforts.

Dietrich Bonhoeffer, a young minister of the German Confessional Church, opposed the rise of the National Socialist Party (Nazis) even before Hitler's rise to power. G. Leibholz, in his "Memoir," noted that Bonhoeffer recognized "that National Socialism was a brutal attempt to make history without God and to found it on the strength of man alone." Leibholz stated further that Bonhoeffer was firmly and rightly convinced that it is a Christian right and duty to oppose any government which is no longer based on natural law and the law of God. Bonhoeffer understood that both liberal theology and secular totalitarianism held in common the idea that the Bible has to be adapted to the requirements of a secular world. According to Leibholz, he believed that, "...the process of debasing Christianity as inaugurated by liberal theology led, in the long run, to a complete perversion and falsification of the essence of Christian teaching by National Socialism." Bonhoeffer further stated that a Christian must be prepared, if

---

[20] Humanist Manifesto I and II, ed. Paul Kurtz, Prometheus Books, 1973

necessary, to offer his life for the rejection of secularism. Therefore, according to Bonhoeffer, "...all kinds of secular totalitarianism which force man to cast aside his religious and moral obligations to God and subordinate the laws of justice and morality to the State are incompatible with his conception of life."[21]

Bonhoeffer was arrested by the Gestapo in 1943, and hanged in April, 1945, by special order of Himmler (second in command to Hitler), just a few days before the concentration camp was liberated by the Allies. His message of opposing the innate injustices and immoralities of any secular government stand as a beacon to all Christians in our current darkening world. American Christians who now watch with antipathy as our government is pulled more and more away from God's laws to the secular system of "justice," must stand convicted by Bonhoeffer's words.

The founding fathers of the United States, more than any group of political thinkers before or after, did produce a workable society based on the principles of personal responsibility and education of the masses. The current arguments being put forth concerning whether the founding fathers intended to produce a society founded on purely secular concepts are, in my opinion, attempts at re-writing history. Clearly the founding fathers understood that there is a God, and that the rights and freedoms of all human beings were and are endowments from that God. Their writings are replete with references to God.

Even Thomas Jefferson, that "rational" Christian who stripped all references of "supernatural" occurrences out of his bible (the first "rational higher critic"?), wrote "We hold these truths to be self-evident, that all men are created equal, that they are endowed by their *Creator* (italics mine) with certain

---

[21] "Memoir," G. Leibholz, in the preface before <u>The Cost of Discipleship</u> (by D. Bonhoeffer), Touchstone, 1995 (Previously published 1959)

unalienable rights. ...We, therefore, the representatives of the United States of America, in General Congress assembled, appealing to the *Supreme Judge* (italics mine) of the world. ...And for the support of this declaration, with a firm reliance on the protection of *Divine Providence,* (italics mine) we mutually pledge to each other our lives, our fortunes, and our sacred honor."[22] Jefferson obviously believed that God did exist, and that mankind owed all our rights to that Creator.

Samuel Adams likewise stated
"'Just and true liberty, equal and impartial liberty,' in matters spiritual and temporal, is a thing that all men are clearly entitled to by the eternal and immutable laws of *God* (italics mine) and nature...In the state of nature every man is, under *God* (italics mine), judge and sole judge of his own rights and of the injuries done him."
Adams further stated in his article entitled, "The Rights Of The Colonists As Christians,"
"These may be best understood by reading and carefully studying the institutes of the great Lawgiver and Head of the Christian Church, which are to be found clearly written and promulgated in the New Testament."[23]

There was an underlying foundational truth for the vast majority of the founding fathers that a government and its society could only function properly when the rules of the government were based on divine principles. To propose a theory that they were trying to formulate a nation totally "free" of all religion is a perversion of their intent that is nothing less than breathtaking. They certainly tried to establish a government which would not advocate one religion over another, but they also clearly never envisioned a government that would rebuke religion, which is, in the end, the goal of secularism.

[22] The Declaration of Independence, Thomas Jefferson, 1776
[23] The Rights of the Colonists As Christians, Samuel Adams, 1772

A discussion of all the wars over religion and repression of religion that ravaged the European nations during the two centuries before the founding of the U.S. is beyond the scope of this work. The results of those wars in Europe were many governments and religions tied to one another. It is clear that the American founding fathers intended to establish a government and society that would allow the free expression of religion without governmental interference. Again, the concept that they were trying to establish a government and society completely free of religion is simply the ultimate perversion of truth.

Unfortunately the humanist concept of "Celebrating Diversity" introduced in the 1990s in the U.S. is helping to reduce the once powerful American "melting pot" into the chaos of "tribalism", as predicted by de Tocqueville in 1835.[24] Celebrating diversity only sounds wonderful, and indeed sounds like something everyone should welcome and aspire to. However, when the fact that "we" are all Americans is de-emphasized, the "melting pot" concept of the first 200 years of the U.S. stops working. When one group begins to think that their ethnic culture supersedes the "common" American culture, tribalist tendencies begin to arise. This once powerful Republic is now becoming a stage for competing tribes to jockey for power.

Even the political parties no longer seem to look to the greater good of the country. Politicians appear ready to do and say anything to gain the upper hand. While others will argue that this has always been the case, I would argue that there have been leaders in the political parties in the past who understood that the good of the country came first. At this time in the history of the U.S., this does not appear to be the case. Those who believe in socialist big government as the "best" way to "care" for its citizens would probably argue that

---

[24] Democracy in America, Alexis de Tocqueville, ed. Richard Heffner, Mentor Book, 1956

33

those humanist administrative and congressional leaders are just trying to bring about these "helpful" changes for the future. But the character of a country is a reflection of the character of its citizens, and a government that enables the weaknesses of its citizens eventually weakens its citizenry, and therefore itself. The continued addition of costly entitlements to our citizens—and non-citizens—continue to pull our country down the rabbit hole of fiscal instability, and all for more power for the current political party, whichever that might be at the time.

Oddly enough, the fall of the U.S. from Superpower to second or third world status does fit into God's plan for this world. The Christian evangelical eschatological vision as given to us through the prophecies of the Bible clearly reveals that there will be a World Government headed by the Anti-Christ, and that there will be a Great Tribulation such as the world has never seen before,

*"For then there will be a great tribulation, such as has not occurred since the beginning of the world until now, nor ever will"* Matthew 24:21

We know that the Tribulation will be followed by the return of Jesus, who will destroy several armies during the battle known as Armageddon. He will then establish a 1000-year world kingdom, with its capital in Jerusalem, known as the Millennial Kingdom. Jesus will rule over the entire world, which will be at peace, and men will live as long as trees live,

*"For as the days of a tree, so will be the days of my people; my chosen ones will long enjoy the work of their hands."* Isaiah 65:22b

While every knee will bow and every tongue confess that Jesus is King, many will do so unwillingly. At the end of the 1000 years (the Millennium), Satan will be released, and lead the rebellious against Jerusalem. God will quickly quash them with fire[25]. The entire surface of the world will be destroyed with fire

*"See, the LORD is going to lay waste the earth and devastate it; he will ruin its face and scatter its inhabitants...The earth will be completely laid waste and totally plundered. The LORD has spoken this word. ...The earth is defiled by its people; they have disobeyed the laws, violated the statutes and broken the everlasting covenant... Therefore earth's inhabitants are burned up, and very few are left."* <u>Isaiah 24: 1-6</u>.

*"But the day of the Lord will come like a thief. The heavens will disappear with a roar; the elements will be destroyed by fire, and the earth and everything in it will be laid bare"* <u>2 Peter 3:10</u>

Then Jesus will present His Father with the Kingdom, the New Jerusalem will descend from above and the earth will be resurrected into the New Earth that we will inhabit for eternity

*"Since everything will be destroyed in this way, what kind of people ought you to be? You ought to live holy and godly lives as you look forward to the day of God and speed its coming. That day will bring about the destruction of the heavens by fire, and the elements will melt in the heat. But in keeping with his promise we are looking forward to a new heaven and a new earth, where righteousness dwells."* <u>2 Peter 3:11-13</u>

*"Then I saw a new heaven and a new earth; for the first heaven and the first earth passed away."* <u>Revelation 21:1</u>

---

[25] <u>The Bible</u>, God through many authors; **"When the thousand years are over, Satan will be released from his prison and will go out to deceive the nations** in the four corners of the earth—Gog and Magog—and to gather them for battle. In number they are like the sand on the seashore. They marched across the breadth of the earth and surrounded the camp of God's people, the city he loves. But **fire came down from heaven and devoured them.** And the devil, who deceived them, was thrown into the lake of burning sulfur, where the beast and the false prophet had been thrown. They will be tormented day and night for ever and ever." <u>Revelation 20:7-10</u>

*"No longer will there be any curse. The throne of God and of the Lamb will be in the city, and his servants will serve him. They will see his face, and his name will be on their foreheads. There will be no more night. They will not need the light of a lamp or the light of the sun, for the Lord God will give them light. And they will reign for ever and ever."* <u>Revelation 22:3-5</u>

These are God's promises to us through Biblical prophecy.

Strangely, most Christians are unaware of the biblical concept of Heaven actually being on the resurrected earth, and seem to think of Heaven as some ethereal place where we will float around on clouds and strum lyres all day. This concept apparently grew out of the ancient Greek philosophers' influence on the early Christian fathers, perhaps best explained by Randy Alcorn in his discussion of Christoplatonism.[26] The Greeks considered spiritual things as good, but material or worldly things were thought of as bad, an ideology and philosophy known as Dualism. They introduced the concept of the "good" spirit trapped in the "evil" body.

The Bible, on the other hand, is very clear that God created the material Earth and called it "Good". Only after the Fall of Adam and Eve was the Curse put on this world.[27] The Bible is also very clear that the future eternal state will be a resurrected New Earth and a New Jerusalem without a Curse. God will live among us, and the conditions and settings will be too wonderful for us to dream of in our current states. Our resurrection bodies will be able to do things that are

---

[26] <u>Heaven</u>, "Appendix A: Christoplatonism's False Assumptions", Randy Alcorn, Tyndale, 2004

[27] <u>The Bible</u>, God through many authors, *To Adam he said, "Because you listened to your wife and ate fruit from the tree about which I commanded you, 'You must not eat from it,' "Cursed is the ground because of you; through painful toil you will eat food from it all the days of your life.* <u>Genesis. 3:17</u> (see also verses 18,19)

36

undreamed of now. Imagine climbing Mount Everest without oxygen or even getting tired!

## JEWISH ESCHATOLOGY:

Jewish eschatological ideas are a little more complex in that each of the three main branches of Judaism approaches the "end times" a little differently. Orthodox Judaism still looks for the Messiah to come and establish Torah (The Law) over all of the earth. The Conservative Jews look to the Messiah only as a metaphor for the establishment of a just and godly human society. Reform Jews have removed all allusions to Messianism. The Orthodox still await Messiah, but there is much discussion whether Messiah will be a human being, or if the Jews as a people will be God's appointed servant. But the traditional Jewish eschatological view has expected Messiah to re-establish the Jewish kingdom on earth.[28]

There is a fourth branch of Judaism, the Messianic Jews. Most of the believing Jews that I have encountered and/or have read their books hold to the evangelical Christian eschatological vision of the Rapture of the Church, followed by the Tribulation, followed by the return of Yeshua (Jesus), and the establishment of the Millennial Kingdom (a Jewish Kingdom), followed by the establishment of Heaven on Earth with the New Jerusalem.

---

[28] What Do Jews Believe, David S. Ariel, Shocken Books, New York,1995

# MUSLIM ESCHATOLOGY:

The other eschatological view that must be mentioned is the Shia Muslim theology. Muslims are divided into two divisions: Shia and Sunni. The difference between the Shia (Shiites) and the Sunni revolves around who can be an Imam, a leader of the faith. The Shia believe that all true Imams must be descendants of Mohammed through his cousin and son-in-law, Ali. Ali married Mohammed's daughter, Fatima, and only their descendants could be called an Imam, according to the Shia. The Sunni believe that the leaders can be chosen. The Shia are further divided by the number of Imams who they believe have come after Ali. Some believe there were Five Imams after Ali, others believe there were Seven Imams, and still others who believe Twelve Imams followed him. These sects are called Fivers, Seveners, and Twelvers. In Iran, the Twelvers hold sway. Twelvers believe that when the eleventh Imam died in 874 A.D., his brother would become Imam because there was no known son.

However, at the funeral a young lad showed up and proclaimed himself the son of the Imam, and thus the Twelfth Imam. This caused a lot of chaos, and then the young man "disappeared" and has not "returned" yet. The belief is that when the time is right, he will appear again as the Mahdi (the divine leader) and will lead the Islamic armies to victory against all enemies and will establish a world-wide Islamic regime. The official Iranian (Shiite) eschatology is capsulated below:

1. The Mahdi is coming soon.
2. The Imam Mahdi is a direct descendant of the prophet Mohammad.
3. He will appear suddenly.
4. A voice from the sky will announce his reappearance at the Holy Ka'ba in Mecca.
5. He will be joined by 313 of the most devoted believers.

6. Only Allah knows the exact time of his appearance on earth.
7. The Mahdi will then travel from Mecca to Medina.
8. Sofyani, an archenemy will attack Syria and Iraq and commit great crimes against humanity in Iraq.
9. The Mahdi will send troops who will kill Sofyani in Jerusalem.
10. Jesus will return and serve as the Mahdi's deputy.
11. The Mahdi will establish his global government with the headquarters in Kufa, Iraq.
12. The Earth will be filled with justice—a global government of peace and justice.
13. All will convert to Islam, which will be the lasting world religion.
14. The world will experience astounding growth in science and technology under the Mahdi's guidance.
15. The earth will experience abundant rain, and vegetation will flourish—an eternal springtime.[29]

As anyone who knows Christian eschatology can tell, there are similarities between the Shiite and Christian eschatological visions. Both have a savior who comes to earth and defeats a despicable enemy, and then the whole earth enters into a period of eternal rest. Christian eschatology had been around for almost 600 years before Mohammed, and one might speculate that the Shiites might have heard the Christian eschatology before the formation of their own. The Shiite eschatology is not taken from the Koran, but rather comes out of tradition. Those Twelvers who await the Mahdi believe that they must throw the world into chaos to hasten his return.

Christian and Jewish eschatological views had been widely divergent under the figurative interpretations of biblical prophecies adopted by the Church during the Middle Ages by

---

[29] The Apocalypse of Ahmadinejad, Mark Hitchcock, Multnomah books, 2007.

such renown Scholastic theologians as Peter Abelard, Peter Lombard, and Thomas Aquinas. This viewpoint of the biblical prophecies regarding the future Divine Kingdom taught that many of those prophecies were merely figurative language. Since the re-establishment of the literal interpretations by the Puritans in the 17th century, and promulgated by fundamentalist Christians beginning in the late 19th century, the Jewish and Christian eschatological visions have once more converged. Many evangelical Christians now believe that there will indeed be a Jewish kingdom with Jesus as King of Kings established on earth for a thousand years, followed by a resurrected Creation and earth which we call heaven. (This is also the understanding of scripture by most messianic Jews.) The story continues from that point forward for eternity.

# CHAPTER 4

# The Olivet Discourse

Jesus (Yeshua in Hebrew) gave us a broad overview of future events in his discussion with his disciples on the Mount of Olives, as described in <u>Matthew 24 and 25, Mark 13</u>, and <u>Luke 21</u>. <u>Luke 17</u> also contains matters of significance to this discussion. As Jesus was coming out of the great Temple on the second day after his triumphal arrival in Jerusalem, he told his disciples that the temple would be destroyed totally. His disciples were astonished and dismayed. They began to question him about when these things would happen and what would be the signs that they were imminent. His answers to those questions have become known as the Olivet Discourse.

Jesus' first recorded prophecy that day was that the temple would be torn down (<u>Matthew 24:2</u>). He told his horrified disciples that no stone would be left upon another. This was fulfilled about 40 years later when the Roman general Titus and his Roman legions ended the Jewish War (66-70 A.D.) by breaching the final inner walls in Jerusalem and attacking the Temple area. Jewish Zealots had positioned themselves in the building, and a fire was started during the intense battle. The temple burned completely, and so hot that all of the huge amount of gold and silver in the walls and ceiling melted and ran down between the stones. Later, the Roman soldiers pulled all of the stones apart supposedly to get to the gold and silver that had run down between the stones. The prophecy from Jesus regarding the temple was then fulfilled.

In the book of Mark, Jesus told his disciples the prophecy of the destruction of the temple. He was sitting on the Mount of Olives opposite the temple. Four of His closest disciples began to question Him privately, asking when would these things happen, and what would be the sign when all of these things would be fulfilled.

Some people in reading this chapter in Matthew say that all of the prophecies were fulfilled when the temple was destroyed. Those who hold to this interpretation of these verses are called Preterists.

However, that could not be the correct interpretation of this section of Scriptures due to the unfulfilled prophecies such as *"nation would rise up against nation, and kingdom against kingdom"* or *"This gospel of the kingdom shall be preached in the whole world as a testimony to all the nations, and then the end will come."* At no time during the forty years following Christ's crucifixion and the ensuing Jewish War would either of the above prophecies be fulfilled. The Roman Empire was very calm during that time except for the Jewish War and Rome's extension into Britain. The prophecy about the gospel being preached in the whole world and *then* the end coming could not be construed to have occurred in that time frame.

Jesus told his disciples not to be deceived, because *"many will come in My name, saying, 'I am the Christ,' and will mislead many."* Matthew 24:5; Mark 13:6; Luke 21:8. Jesus was saying that in the "End times" there would be many "false" messiahs who would lead people astray. In the last 50 years, we have seen Jim Jones (1978), David Korech (1993), plus many smaller groups (Heaven's Gate, 1997) leading people astray by promising that they were the Messiah. As bad as these leaders were, they are only the foreshadowing of the ones to come. The worst will be the Anti-Christ and his Prophet, who will lead most of the world's population into apostasy.

After describing the signs that they should remain alert for, He used the parable of the Fig Tree, alerting them to watch and be aware when they begin to gather. These signs could be divided into three divisions: First, the signs of the beginning of the End Times, then the historical streams that would continue to strengthen and swell, and finally, the climatic happenings followed by His return to this world.

The signs, or Fig Leaves as the signs are called in this book, are divided as follows:

First, the signs of the beginnings of the era:

Fig Leaf #1:        War: Nation against Nation, Kingdom against Kingdom

Fig Leaves #2,3,4:   Earthquakes, Famines and Plague

Next, the signs of the historical movements that carry mankind into the climax of the era, known as the Tribulation:

Fig Leaf #5:        Hatred and Persecution of Christians

Fig Leaf #6:        Apostasy of the Church

Fig Leaf #7:        False Prophets

Fig Leaves #8,9:    Lawlessness and Love Grown Cold

Fig Leaf #10:       Gospel Preached to All the World

Then comes the climactic Tribulation events of the End Times:

Fig Leaf #11:    The Abomination of Desolation

Fig Leaf #12:    The Great Tribulation

Fig Leaf #13:    The Day of the Lord

Fig Leaf #14:    The Sign of the Lord/The Second
Coming

# Fig Leaf # 1:

# WAR: Nation v. Nation,

# Kingdom v. Kingdom

*"Nation will rise against nation, and kingdom against kingdom."* <u>Matthew 24:7a</u>

Jesus said that before the End Times would come, first *"nation would rise up against nation, and kingdom against kingdom"* <u>Mark 13:8; Luke 21:10</u>. While this might apply to any of the many wars fought in the last 2000 years, there is an implication in His wording that many nations would be involved in the war that would mark the beginning of the End Times. The vast majority of the wars over mankind's past history were fought between 2 countries or kingdoms. While the Thirty Years War in Europe in the 1600s involved many nations/countries, the historical streams of the times do not indicate a major break from previous eras. Also, the Napoleonic wars involved several nations, but again without indications that the any of the other Fig Leaves were showing up.

Many people who have looked at these prophetic sayings are convinced that this probably refers to World War I. For the first time in world history, a war was started first by two nations, Austria and Serbia, and then all of their allies were pulled into the war, erupting into the first war that eventually involved almost every nation in the world. First, Austria declared war on Serbia after Arch-Duke Ferdinand was assassinated (1914). Then, all of the other European countries were dragged into the war due to alliance agreements, and soon the world was at war. First nation against nation, Austria against Serbia, then kingdoms (alliances) against kingdoms (alliances) as Jesus had said. By the end of the war, there were 42 countries fighting with the Allies, and 17 countries allied as the Central Powers. All in all, 59 of the world's 87 countries were involved in the war that had battle sites in Western Europe, Eastern Europe, the Middle East, Italy, Africa, and the Balkans. Sea battles were fought all around the globe. At the end of the war, there were over 17 million deaths resulting from the conflict.

People at the end of World War I thought that it was the "Great War", the "War to end all other wars". Unfortunately, only 21 years later, Germany invaded Poland and the world was thrown into the most costly and wide-spread war ever--World War II. Once again, we saw nation against nation and kingdom against kingdom. Germany allied with Japan and Italy (the Axis powers) against the rest of the world. Battles were fought all across Europe, large parts of Asia, the Pacific islands, and Africa. Never before in the history of mankind had a war involved so many people and so many battle areas. An estimated 70-80 million people died as a result of World War II. Only in the twentieth century, and never before had almost 100 million people died as a result of war. *"For nation will rise against nation, and kingdom against kingdom...but all these things are merely the beginning of birth pangs."* Matthew 24:7a-8. These two wars—considered to be merely parts 1 and 2 of a single devastating war by many historians—seem to meet the description of the first Fig Leaf.

Several important historical streams were forming at the beginning of the twentieth century. Changes in cultural mores, Christian theology, political ideology, scientific progress, as well as the Jewish quest for a homeland began to emerge and strengthen during that era of time. The other Fig Leaves indicating the beginning of the End Times began to show up, and the Fig Leaves indicating the emergence of historical movements that would move Mankind away from the traditional Christian foundations of the last millennium were also showing up and getting gradually stronger.


## Christian Theology

Christian theology began to change in the late 1800s. This will be discussed in detail later under the section on the Apostasy of the Church. Liberal theology, riding on the tide of rational higher criticism of the Scriptures was building into a crescendo during this period of time. Theologians were beginning to doubt the veracity of the ancient church fathers' analysis and interpretation of Scripture. Heresies were beginning to move into the Church. This historical stream that will eventually lead to the apostate church was begun around the turn of the twentieth century.

## Zionism

Not only was theological thinking in the Church changing, but the Jewish quest for their own homeland began to build and modern Zionism was born. In the event known as the First Aliyah, about 25,000 Jews from Russia and Yemen immigrated into that section of southern Syria now known as Israel. They bought land and established several towns from 1880 to 1904. However, due to the severity of the conditions there, almost half of them left before World War I began. During the Second Aliyah, from 1904 to 1914, about 35,000 Russian Jews bought land and immigrated into the area. They started the Kibbutz concept and for the most part, stayed.

Theodor Herzl, an Austrian journalist, had observed the severe anti-Semitism of the Dreyfus Case in Paris in 1894. He realized that anti-Semitism could not be ended with mere words. He became convinced that the Jews had to have their own homeland, and organized the first World Zionist Congress in Basel, Switzerland in 1897. He made efforts within the Ottoman Empire to obtain land for Jews in the southern part of Syria where Jerusalem was located. His efforts with the Ottoman Sultan were mostly ineffective in gaining access to that land. In 1903, British Christian Zionists offered to give 5000 square miles in Africa, in the area of current Uganda, to the World Zionist Congress for a new Jewish homeland. This offer was formally declined in 1905. Hertzl's efforts finally came to fruition in 1917, during World War I when the Ottomans were defeated and England was given the Mandate to administer that area of the world. Jews around the world began to buy land in the area called "Palestine" by the English, and began to move there.

## Technology

From a technological standpoint, the turn of the twentieth century marks the birth of automobiles and airplanes. From WWI forward, the gasoline engine began to be produced in large quantities, and the infrastructure for gasoline distribution was put into place. This pushed many nations into seeking sites where crude oil could be obtained. The British had discovered a large oil field in Persia (now Iran) in 1908, and oil would be discovered in Saudi Arabia in 1938. This technology would rapidly improve the ability of people to travel to foreign lands, and the ability to visit previously unreachable areas of the world. Pursuit of oil would change the way countries interacted in the 20th century.

After World War II, the invention and development of transistors, semiconductors, and integrated circuits led to the rapid growth of the computer and electronics industry. Today, people use small handheld telephones and personal computers that would boggle the minds of the generation that lived through World War II. The rapid growth of these technologies over a hundred year span certainly accentuates the words given to the prophet Daniel:

*"But Daniel, keep this prophecy a secret; seal it up so that it will not be understood until the end times, when travel and education shall be vastly increased."* Daniel 12:4

## Economics

Economically, the socialist/communist theories of Karl Marx as set forth in his three-volume book, *Das Kapital*, were taking hold among intellectuals in Europe—especially after the revolution in Russia in 1917. Capitalism, without regulations, was fostering hardships and oppression among the working class in the mid 1800s. The theories of Marx were being studied during that time, and many intellectuals thought these theories would be the salvation of the oppressed and mankind in general. They seemed to miss the importance of the middle class that capitalism had fostered during the same period of time. But socialism and communism as economic and political systems took root and were being touted as viable replacements for the capitalist systems of the era.

## Politics

On the political front, the Russian Revolution of 1917 shook up the world and gave socialists and communists around the globe a platform to trumpet their ideology to all who would listen. And many people around the world began to listen. The original revolution against the Tsar that started in February of that year was overtaken by Lenin and the communists in October. The following civil war was won by the communists and the great experiment that eventually proved the folly of communism as a governmental and national strategy was born. However the ideology flourished among intellectuals around the world who were beginning to reject the underlying Judeo-Christian moral and judicial foundational base of the European and American governments.

One such center of communism/socialism was the Institute for Social Reform started at Frankfort University in Germany after WWI. This institute gathered together such men as Horkheimer, Fromm and Marcuse. Since most, if not all, of them were Jewish, they fled Germany in the early 1930s when Hitler became Chancellor, and they eventually landed in New York, associated with Columbia University. They became known as the Frankfurt School during that time. While most returned to Germany after WWII, Marcuse remained in the U.S. and became a muse to many of the Baby Boomer generation who rebelled against the "Status Quo" in the 1960s. Marcuse's book, *Eros and Civilization*, stimulated many to rebel against the sexual mores of the day, and his essay, "Repressive Tolerance" (1965), explicitly propounds acceptance of ideas from the Left, but repression of any discussion from the Right. This concept has taken root and seems to be the basis of the philosophical concepts of many politicians, college professors, and media producers throughout Europe and the U.S. today. Even the concepts of "Political Correctness" and the new "Tolerance" draw heavily on this Marcusean philosophy.

Many of the politicians today are Baby Boomers, or educated by Baby Boomers, and have accepted Socialism as a more "humane" system for improving the human condition. Judeo-Christian values are demeaned and actually denigrated as being intolerant and "hateful." One senior U.S. Senator, who ran for President in 2016, has charged during an open Senate committee hearing, that a political appointee was not fit for government service due to the Christian statements made in his (the appointee's) own church. The Senator's charge against the Christian was that he would not be able to be fair to non-Christians.

### Science

Science also began to change during the era of World War I. The concepts of evolution set forth by Charles

Darwin's book, *On the Origin of the Species*, began to be accepted in the scientific community. Darwin had known very little about genetics, since his contemporary, Gregor Mendel had not convinced the scientific community of the merit of his work at that time. Mendel's experimental work with genetics was "rediscovered" by accepted scientists and published in 1900. His concepts of "genes" being able to transmit characteristics from the parents to their progeny became the standard scientific understanding. In the 1920s and 1930s, Darwin's concept of natural selection was synthesized with mutation theory and Mendelian inheritance to form the new Evolution Synthesis theory that is the basis of much scientific knowledge today. This movement toward "natural" causes began to grow in the scientific community, and by the beginning of the 21st century, formal science had discarded any nods toward a creative God. Any scientist in the modern world who acknowledges a Judeo-Christian God may be mocked and will probably have difficulty procuring an academic position. (See *"Expelled, No Intelligence Allowed"*, a documentary video by Ben Stein, 2008)

The "Molecule to Man" concepts are the only scientific teaching allowed in most public schools. Subsequently, the number of children being taught the concepts of the Ten Commandments are diminishing year by year. And the violence in schools and homes by our younger people is also increasing. Yet no one in authority can understand why this might be happening. Those without eyes cannot see, and those without ears cannot hear.

These strands of history set the stage for the growth of Humanism that began to degrade the Christian base of the Western world after the chaos, carnage and mayhem of the two World Wars. During the same time frame the roots for the establishment of Israel were set in place.

# Fig Leaves #2, #3, and #4

# Earthquakes,

# Famines and Plagues

*"There will be great earthquakes, famines and pestilences in various places, and fearful events and great signs from heaven."* <u>Luke 21:11</u>

*"There will be famines and earthquakes in various places."* <u>Matthew 24:7b</u>

There is no doubt that the magnitude of damage of earthquakes is increasing. Earthquakes occur all over the world almost hourly (See *www.earthquake.usgs.gov*). Whether these are more intense and more frequent is difficult to say, due to the paucity of records and methodologies prior to the twentieth century. However, it is safe to say that the world is suffering major earthquakes every year, and due to the increased population of the world, the results are certainly more devastating than in the past. The largest earthquake that has creditable reports occurred in the year 1556 in Shensi Province, China and killed an estimated 830,000 people.

However, since World War I and World War II, there have been multiple earthquakes that have devastated and killed massive numbers of people:
Tangshan, China in 1976 (over 250,000-650,000 killed);
Sumatra in 2004 (over 250,000 killed by the tsunami);
Kashmir 2005 (75,500 killed);
Sichuan, China 2008 (about 80,000 killed);
Haiti in 2010 (over 250,000 killed);
Tohoku, Japan (15,000 killed in tsunami and Fukushima nuclear plant disaster);

Nepal 2015 (9000 killed and 3 million homeless).

These twentieth and twenty-first century earthquakes have resulted in the deaths of over one and a half million people.

If we consider all of the natural disasters in our generation, we see the damage done by hurricanes (i.e. Katrina in 2005), tornadoes, wildfires, volcanoes, snow storms, floods, etc., and the great human casualties in those disasters. Again whether there are more disasters now than in the past is debatable, but we know that the damage is much worse due to the population increases and the concentration of the populations into smaller areas than in the past.

In the same verse above that foretells increasing earthquakes, He mentions plagues. Throughout the history of the world, the term "plague" has brought to mind Bubonic Plague. History tells us about two great bubonic plague scourges that occurred prior to the 20th century. The first was the Plague of Justinian that devastated the Byzantine world during 541-542 A.D, killing 15-25 million people. Next was the Black Death that killed approximately one third of the European population from 1346 to 1353. A third outbreak of bubonic plague was called the Third Pandemic, which began in China in 1855, spread to almost all of the inhabited continents, and killed over 12 million people in India and China alone. It was finally considered over in 1959.

But other plagues arose in the 20th century. In the same year that World War I came to an end, 1918, there occurred a world-wide plague caused by influenza. This has come to be called the Great Flu Epidemic of 1918. It infected approximately 500 million people around the world, and killed somewhere between 50 to 100 million of those, making it the most deadly pandemic in history.

The Asian Flu Pandemic of 1957-1958 killed about 2 million people globally while the Hong Kong flu a decade later killed about 1 million around the world.

There have been seven cholera pandemics in the world since 1819. The last two occurred in the 20$^{th}$ century with the last one ending in 1966. Well over a million lives were lost to this disease in the 20$^{th}$ century alone.

Typhus has caused many deaths over the centuries, but 3 million Russians died in the epidemic lasting from 1918 to 1922. Another 3.5 million Russian soldiers died from typhus while interred in Nazi prisoner of war camps during WWII.

While treatment has been available for tuberculosis since the late 1940s, this disease was responsible for killing over 100 million people in the 20$^{th}$ century.

We have seen a new disease arise called AIDS (1981) that has decimated most of Africa and many other countries. The world's culture has changed tremendously since the 1960s. Sexual freedom and promiscuity is now the cultural norm in the Western world. The Gay assault has likewise desensitized these societies against God's warnings about consequences of these lifestyles. AIDS is running amok through African societies and others that promote a culture of wife swapping and free sex. Unfortunately the disease is spreading also to the innocent--children and health care workers. The World Health Organization has estimated that over 35 million people have died from AIDS from 1981 to 2014. They estimate that another 35 million are infected.

The SARS virus outbreak began in Asia in 2003 and spread worldwide, killing thousands before dying down.

In 2009, the "Swine" flu (H1N1) began in Mexico and spread around the world causing much illness and death. This was a strain similar to the flu strain that killed millions in 1918. The estimated global death count was around 285,000.

In 1976, the Ebola virus was identified, and between then and 2013, 24 outbreaks were identified with just under 2000 cases. In December 2013, the large outbreak in western Africa began. When finally contained in the spring of 2016, it had infected about 29,000 people and caused about 11,320 deaths.

The Zika virus began to be recognized in the 1950s in Africa. It made its way across Africa to Asia by the 1980s. Then it moved into Polynesia, and by 2015 was found in the Americas. As of 2018, there is no vaccine against it. While Zika has not caused any known deaths, it is the cause of microcephaly in babies of infected mothers.

We are being warned about the next epidemic, the "Bird Flu" which seems to be looming in Asia, waiting to get a human host before spreading all around the world, killing millions again.

Another developing problem are "superbug" infections. More and more bacteria are becoming resistant to our current antibiotics. We have not been able to develop enough new antibiotics to stay ahead of this problem. Many infectious disease experts are predicting that these infections will become more prevalent and possibly rampant in the near future.

Since World War I, almost 150 million people have died from plagues. Certainly, we can say that this Fig Leaf is here now.

Famine completes the verse. In the 20th century more than 70 million people died around the world due to famine. Two of the most horrendous famines were caused by the communist policies in Russia and China.

Although about 2 million Russians had died in the 1922 famine caused by a severe drought, another estimated 6-8 million people died in the 1932-1933 famine caused by Stalin's new agricultural policies. Most of those who died were Ukrainians. Due to the intense secrecy of the political regime at the time, and the favorable bias from Western journalists, the exact number of deaths has never been accurately reported.

The other great famine occurred in China from 1959 to 1961. Again exact numbers of deaths were difficult to obtain due to the desire of the ruling regime to suppress them. As in Russia, this famine has been blamed on the interaction of drought conditions with the policies of the communist regime. The estimated number of deaths has been placed at somewhere between 50 to 75 million people.

From 1967 to 1970, over 3 million people in the eastern Nigerian section of Biafra died from starvation due to the war of secession being raged. All imports into the area were embargoed, and the people could not raise enough food to feed themselves.

Communism was again the culprit of the famine in North Korea from 1994 to 1998. Again accurate numbers are not available, but estimates of starvation-related deaths have ranged from 300,000 to 3.5 million out of a total population of 22 million people.

Drought in many of the agricultural sections of Ethiopia in the mid-1980s also resulted in many deaths. The main economic machine of the Ethiopian economy is agriculture. The government during this period of time used a large part of the national treasure to keep a large standing army due to the ongoing attacks throughout the country by communist terrorists. Subsequently, even with help from the U.N., it has been estimated that about 500,000 people died from the famine.

Drought and war combined again in 1998 in southwestern Sudan to produce a famine that killed over

70,000 people—again in spite of humanitarian efforts from the rest of the world.

The world community has become aware of famines, and mechanisms have been set in place to help victims. However, with much of our grain crops around the world going into fuel production, we may actually begin to see food shortages increase.

These were the beginnings of the "birth pangs". These things are just the signs of the beginning of the End Times. We could say that they have been fulfilled already, but more of each is yet to come. During the Tribulation, the Anti-Christ will carry out several terrible wars, earthquakes will continue to worsen as described in the Bible, and plagues and famine will kill multitudes of people. So these signs are only partially fulfilled at this time.

# Fig Leaf #5:

# Hatred and Persecution

*"Then you will be handed over to be persecuted and put to death, and you will be hated by all nations because of me."* Matthew 24:9

Jesus tells us of hatred of anyone who follows after Him. This hatred is evident all over the world. Christians in China and Viet Nam are hounded, imprisoned, and killed for their faith. In Muslim countries like Pakistan, Sudan, Egypt, and Indonesia, Christians are persecuted and oppressed by the people and governments to the point of death. In Saudi Arabia and other Muslim countries under Sharia law, Christians are not allowed to worship God at all. In Egypt, members of the ancient Christian church have been under government and cultural pressure to become Muslim for many decades. Christians must pay very high taxes compared to Muslims. Muslim terrorists attack and kill Christians frequently. The church has been driven out of Iraq since the establishment of its new government following Desert Storm in the early 1990s. The Muslims are not the only religious sect to hate Christians. Hindus kill many Christians every year, as well as any missionaries who would try to bring them knowledge of Jesus. Please go to the website of the Voice of the Martyrs at www.persecutions.com to read about the persecution of Christians worldwide.

In Europe, Christianity is seemingly considered more like a club affiliation than an integral part of a person's life. During the Middle Ages, the Roman popes wielded supreme power over the people and their rulers. Many pagan and superstitious beliefs were brought into the Church, and anyone who did not believe the Church dogma was declared a heretic, and subject to be burned alive. Anyone who angered a pope or bishop could be ex-communicated from the Church. Because the Church had brought in the non-Biblical teaching that anyone not in communion with the Church at the time of death could not get into heaven, people—both common and royal—were afraid not to adhere to the clerical mandates. The popes had declared that personal opinion and public dissention with the Church would result in that person's excommunication, and therefore denial to access to heaven in the afterlife. After the era of the Enlightenment, and the formation of the United States and its constitutional proclamation of free speech and thinking in the early 1800s, the concept of freedom and personal beliefs became a common right of people in the U.S., and began to foster the same concepts in areas around the world. The importance of adhering to Church dogma began to lessen, and many Europeans began to question the legitimacy of that dogma. Subsequently, with the growth of humanism in Europe, Christianity has become a non-factor in most of the people's lives.

In the U.S., Christians are constantly criticized by progressive liberal groups. The progressive lies and libels are then echoed through the main media outlets without any apparent journalistic filtering at all. The U.S. court system has adopted the perverted version of the First Amendment that essentially is trying to drive religion out of the "public view." All in all, Christians in America seem to be fair game and easy targets for the secular society and its media and political mouthpieces. The apostles all knew that this was coming in the future.

Peter warned that *"...in the last days mockers will come with their mocking, following after their own lusts, and saying, 'Where is the promise of His coming? For ever since the fathers fell asleep, all continues just as it was from the beginning of creation.'"* 2 Peter 3:3-4

59

*"Therefore, dear friends, since you have been forewarned, be on your guard so that you may not be carried away by the error of the lawless and fall from your secure position. ..."* 2 Peter 3:17

Paul warned that *"...in the last days difficult times will come...among them (unscrupulous men) are those who enter into households and captivate weak women weighed down with sins, led on by various impulses, always learning and never able to come to the knowledge of the truth...so these men also oppose the truth, men of depraved mind, rejected in regard to the truth."* 2 Timothy 3:1,6,7,8

Jude warned that *"...(we) ought to remember the words that were spoken beforehand by the apostles of our Lord Jesus Christ, that they were saying to you, 'In the last time there will be mockers, following after their own ungodly lusts.' These are the ones who cause divisions, worldly-minded, devoid of the Spirit."* Jude 17-19

Clearly Jesus had warned the apostles, and they have warned us about this growing hatred against those who love God and His Word.  It is not only the hatred, but the mocking and disrespect for Christianity by non-believers that continues to grow.  As the number of people who embrace humanism grows in numbers, Christians will be singled out as backward and anti-progressive.  Public opinion will be turned against Christianity and its followers.

While the movement against Christianity will come primarily from outside of its membership, many inside the Church will begin to have doubts and begin to question doctrine.  This will give rise to the Apostate Church.

Jesus informed us that this dislike will become hatred and will continue to grow.  Finally, when the Anti-Christ comes to power during the Tribulation, anyone who comes to Christ will be persecuted and most likely killed.

# Fig Leaf #6:

# Apostasy of the Church

*"At that time many will turn away from the faith and will betray and hate each other"* <u>Matthew 24:10</u>

The next sign of the coming of the End Times is apostasy. This refers to people who say they believe in the Gospel, but then "fall away." Jesus warns that many will fall away from the true faith and begin to follow false prophets. We are seeing this on a large scale both here in the U.S., and without argument, in Europe. In the late 1800s and up through World War I, new arguments about the origins of the biblical scriptures were introduced to the world through the writings of Wellhausen (Documentary Hypothesis) and Bultmann (Form Criticism). The essence of these new theories was that the Bible books were not written by the authors that the church fathers had ascribed to them, but rather they were collections of Jewish ideas that were put down by scribes usually much later in the case of most of the Old Testament scriptures, and also some of the New Testament. Subsequently, many of the Biblical teachings came under "suspicion" of being human inventions.

Thus within several mainstream churches, there exists a liberal faction that has promoted the idea that the literal interpretation of the Bible is naïve, and supernatural events such as the Virgin Birth may not have actually happened. Since the early 1900s, there have been questions raised by these scholars about its historical accuracy. "The doctrine of the virgin birth, as it is called, has been asserted, doubted, and denied by men who all equally claim to be loyal followers of

Jesus."[30]  These concepts are taught in many seminaries which are preparing the shepherds for God's sheep.  If the shepherds present such concepts and raise doubts about the Scriptures, then many of the sheep are going to follow along.

People in some mainstream denominations are given the option of picking and choosing what they believe is true in the Bible.  The result has been a massive "falling away" by the members of those churches.

One example we can use is the Church of England.  It remains the state church of that country, so technically anyone living there can enroll in the Church membership.  While a review of church statistics is difficult to decipher regarding membership numbers, we can certainly look at the number of confirmations in the last one hundred years.  According to published church records, confirmations have fallen tremendously over that period of time as follows: In 1910, there were 227,000 confirmations; 113,000 in 1970; 60,000 in 1990; and 36,000 in 2000.[31]  (It would not be fair to isolate the Church of England in this regard, since baptisms in almost all, if not all, major denominations have been decreasing steadily in the West.  However, some Anglican priests have been very prominent in voicing their negative views regarding the historical accuracy of the Gospels, the Virgin Birth, and even the Resurrection.  At least one has even stated that he was an atheist, but was still a priest in the church.  However, in defense of the Church of England, recordings from recent Synods have been very critical of clergy who teach heresy such as no virgin birth or resurrection).

According to the <u>Abingdon Commentary for Twentieth Century Christians,</u> even the twenty-fourth chapter of

[30]<u>Abingdon Commentary for Twentieth Century Christians;</u> "The Life of Jesus Christ" by Joseph McFadyen, p. 891; Frederick Carl Eiselen, ed. Doubleday and Co. 1929

[31] www.cofe.anglican.org/info/statistics

Matthew, called the Olivet Discourse, which we are discussing here, was also considered to be mostly Jewish eschatological ideas placed in the text by whoever wrote down these scriptures, and contained very little of Jesus' own words or ideas.[32]

In the 1960s, Secular Christians and Christian Atheists such as Paul van Buren, Gabriel Vahanian, and Thomas J.J. Altizer spearheaded the "God is dead" movement, in which they explored the different aspects of modern mankind's rejection of the "Biblical God".[33],[34],[35] Episcopal Bishop Spong wrote about being a "believer in exile" and asserted that Christianity had to change to remain relevant to our culture.[36] His books are still being sold in bookstores today.

And of course the famous Jesus Seminar continues to publish its reports to the delight of the secular press. The members of this organization—most of whom are scholars, and some of whom are not—vote on whichever section of New Testament scripture they are "studying" by dropping colored balls into a basket. One color means they believe Jesus actually said that particular phrase, while another color indicates they do not believe Jesus said it. Thus by democratic

[32] Abingdon Commentary for Twentieth Century Christians; Frederick Carl Eiselen, ed. Doubleday and Co. 1929: "*The author of this Gospel must remain unknown. The reason why Matthew's name has been linked with it is because of a saying of Papias quoted in Eusebius....The compiler of the Gospel was evidently a Jew of the Dispersion who lived outside of Palestine...*" Page 955; "*Few modern interpreters believe that the whole discourse can be attributed to Jesus...support the theory that the chapter is a composite structure made up of genuine sayings of Jesus and a Jewish/Christian apocalypse.*" Page 1014

[33] The Gospel of Christian Atheism, Thomas J.J. Altizer, Philadelphia, Westminster, 1966

[34] The Death of God, Gabriel Vahanian, George Braziller, 1961

[35] The Secular Meaning of the Gospels: An Analysis of its Language, Paul van Buren, Pelican, 1963

[36] Why Christianity Must Change or Die, John Shelby Spong, HarperCollins, 1998

vote, they decide if the scripture is "authentic."[37] Unfortunately, these are the "Biblical scholars" that the press most often interview when they need a Christian point of view. Because of these assaults on the veracity of the Scriptures over the past century, the belief in the inerrancy of the Scriptures has slipped tremendously.

It becomes very easy then for heretical teachers to gain traction among Christians, because most churches today do not disciple their members. (Discipling would involve teaching orthodox theology and promoting and encouraging spiritual growth through reading and discussing the great Christian classics as well as the Bible.) Since Church members are not taught orthodoxy, they are not armed to discern heresy when it shows up. With the great numbers of people in America and Europe who have been exposed, and perhaps, indoctrinated with humanism and secularism, the churches are beginning to see marked decreases in the number of people who profess Christ.

Leaders of the various denominations will begin to foster ecumenicalism as a sign of God's love for all people. This in-gathering of multiple theologies will allow the heresies to gain new followers, and orthodox theology will begin to diminish in acceptance among the church leaders and members.

All of this is foreshadowing of the Great Apostasy that will come with the Anti-Christ and his Prophet. This apostate "Church" will be an ecumenical organization that will strive to be inclusive for almost anyone who might want to join. Beliefs and creeds will not be a problem. These "enlightened" church members will willingly expose those people who hold to the old-fashioned ideas of fundamental Christianity. Church priests will seek out any whose beliefs do not line up with the

---

[37] The New Evidence That Demands a Verdict, Josh McDowell, Thomas Nelson Publishers, 1999, Chap. 29, pp. 562-564.

dogma of the new Church. Orthodox Christians will be scrutinized, mocked, denigrated publicly, and eventually turned over to the secular government justice system for punishment. These punishments will become more and more severe. By the time the Apostate Church is brought into the World Religion, the punishment will be death.

We have seen the type, or foreshadowing, for this activity in the Inquisition of the Roman Catholic Church. The Inquisition has resulted in the deaths of hundreds of thousands of people since the 15th century who simply held a different belief than Catholic dogma. Jews, Muslims, and Protestants have been deprived of their property, dignity, and lives because they would not follow the tenets of the Catholic Church. In the same way, anyone who will not accept the Anti-Christ as his/her savior in that soon-coming false religion will be tortured and killed.

# Fig Leaf #7:

# False Prophets

*"Many false prophets will appear and deceive many people."* <u>Matthew 24:11</u>

Jesus's warning about the false messiahs and their deceptions would be the next "fig leaf". Many people are claiming special insights, and leading people astray. They gather together people who are looking for more than our culture and world can offer. We are seeing a marked increase in "spirituality" as an attribute to be desired. Many people are now looking to Buddhism or New Age Spirituality to try to fill the empty "God-space" inside of them. The pantheism of the Native American culture is resurging, and being mimicked by the New Agers. The silliness of arranging furniture to provide a more "restful" or "calming" environment (feng shui) would have been laughed out of the house in the early 20<sup>th</sup> century, but is strong among today's secularists. Even for Christians, there are those "leaders" who gather people (and their money) together in the name of Jesus, and then begin teaching false doctrine. The previous section on Fig Leaf #6 discussed several church thought-leaders who have brought heretical teachings into the church, leading to apostasy.

Fortunately, many people <u>are</u> still finding that our Lord is the way to true peace and joy, but our churches are remaining lukewarm in getting the gospel to the lost in America.

As God's plan for the world continues to move forward and humanism becomes more and more prominent among mankind, the culture will become more accommodating for false teachers. Leaders from the various religions will begin to find common ground in order to bring more and more people together, eventually leading to the World Religion.

Peter also warned about the false teachers.

*"But there were also false prophets among the people, just as there will be false teachers among you. They will secretly introduce destructive heresies, even denying the sovereign Lord who bought them—bringing swift destruction on themselves. Many will follow their depraved conduct and will bring the way of truth into disrepute. In their greed these teachers will exploit you with fabricated stories. Their condemnation has long been hanging over them, and their destruction has not been sleeping"* 2 Peter 2:1-3

Peter recognized and warned about those "teachers" who spout heresies in order to gain wealth and fame. There are many who masquerade as Christians in our culture today. Others just promote ideas that will supposedly make their followers rich, or feel good about themselves, or just sound plausible. Peter also knew that the outcome of these heresies is eternal separation from God.

*"Dear friends, although I was very eager to write to you about the salvation we share, I felt compelled to write and urge you to contend for the faith that was once for all entrusted to God's holy people.*

*For certain individuals whose condemnation was written about long ago have secretly slipped in among you. They are ungodly people, who pervert the grace of our God into a license for immorality and deny Jesus Christ our only Sovereign and Lord.*

*These people are grumblers and faultfinders; they follow their own evil desires; they boast about themselves and flatter others for their own advantage.*

*But, dear friends, remember what the apostles of our Lord Jesus Christ foretold. They said to you, "In the last times there will be scoffers who will follow their own ungodly desires." These are the people who divide you, who follow mere natural instincts and do not have the Spirit."* Jude 3-4; 16-19

Jude also was aware of the danger of these teachers who proclaim God, but are really just promoting themselves. These people will become more and more prominent as the world moves away from the Truth of God.

Paul noted that the time will come when the people themselves will promote false teachers.

*"For the time will come when people will not put up with sound doctrine. Instead, to suit their own desires, they will gather around them a great number of teachers to say what their itching ears want to hear. They will turn their ears away from the truth and turn aside to myths."* 2 Timothy 4:3-4

Why will people start to turn from Truth? As people are indoctrinated into the concepts that there is no God, and therefore there is no absolute truth, they will begin searching for something to hold on to. Blaise Pascal had written about this longing in his collection of theological and philosophical essays entitled *Pensees (Thoughts)* in the 17th century. The English paraphrase has become known as the "God-shaped hole in the heart." "But if God is not there, then people will search for something they hope will fill it. But if it is not from God's Word, their search will be in vain."

Paul further expounded on the nature of people in the End Times.

*"But mark this: There will be terrible times in the last days. People will be lovers of themselves, lovers of money, boastful, proud, abusive, disobedient to their parents, ungrateful, unholy, without love, unforgiving, slanderous, without self-control, brutal, not lovers of the good, treacherous, rash, conceited, lovers of pleasure rather than lovers of God—having a form of godliness but denying its power. Have nothing to do with such people."* 2 Timothy 3:1-5

While humanism does not necessarily teach egoism, it has nothing in its repertoire that would discourage self-absorption. People without God in their heart will fill it with themselves and the things that they think will increase their own self-worth (usually money and/or power).

False teachers will prey on inwardly turned people. People who live for themselves without regard for others bring discord into their own lives and the lives of those around them. A world filled with these people will bring about the lawless and cold culture of the End Times.

# Fig Leaf #8 and #9:

# Lawlessness & Love Grown Cold

*"Because lawlessness is increased, most people's love will grow cold."* <u>Matthew 24: 12</u>

In verse twelve of Matthew 24, Jesus noted that lawlessness will increase. I don't think anyone can deny that the percentage of law-abiding people in this country is decreasing. When I was a child, there was nothing wrong in talking to strangers, meeting people I didn't know, or walking all over town any time of day or night. Today, children are taught not to talk to strangers, and are driven everywhere by their parents, who then must watch over them in public places due to the increase in lawless people who might kidnap or otherwise harm them. Television shows and movies depict people doing horrible things to others, desensitizing viewers to the horrors of mayhem and murder. Even the "heroes" of these shows have issues with obeying laws. Overall, the respect for law is dropping even among so-called "law-abiding" citizens. Certainly the argument can be made that this lawlessness is directly affected by the loss of Judeo-Christian values around the country. As Humanism increases, and Christianity recedes, this will continue to be a growing problem.

Because of the lawlessness, Jesus noted that people's *"love will grow cold."* <u>Matthew 24:12</u> As we become afraid of strangers, we become less willing to help those we do not know. We also are less willing to help strangers who come to our doors. Hitchhiking has become almost impossible because most people are afraid to pick up a stranger on the side of the road. As our fear increases—due to increasing lawlessness—our love for others (and more specifically, strangers) decreases. Jesus' parable of the Good Samaritan cuts deep into our hearts today because of our fear to help others.

There is another influence on the increasing coldness in the hearts of the people: the Internet effect. Due to the anonymity that people can use on the internet, the loss of civility has increased tremendously. Some of the "trolling" that occurs on-line is done more in a humorous intent, but quite a lot is vitriolic and vicious. This is being done for religious reasons, political reasons, and personal reasons. But the overall effect is to harden the hearts of those attacked resulting in vitriolic counterattacks.

One of the favorite methodologies of those who use this technique to diminish those who do not think like them is the "Broad Brush." Among other issues, an example would be anyone who questions how much humankind is contributing to the warming of the climate. He/She would be labelled as a climate change denier by the Broad Brushers without regard to any factual information provided. It does not matter to those who throw this epithet at others whether their victim(s) agree that the climate is warming, but question if some other natural phenomenon might be causative. The Broad Brush is used to try to shame and silence any opposition to mainstream thought. The Broad Brush can be made even broader in this particular subject by accusing their victim(s) of being "anti-scientific."

No longer can people engage in debate about issues in a civil manner. The Broad Brushers are not interested in finding Truth because they only want to impose their own thoughts on everyone else.

# Fig Leaf #10:

# Gospel Preached in the Whole World

*"This gospel of the kingdom shall be preached in the whole world as a testimony to all the nations, and then the end will come."* <u>Matthew 24:14</u>

Jesus then stated that after the Gospel is preached in the whole world, the end will come. Only since the beginning of the twentieth century has the ability to go to the ends of the world with translated Bibles been so available. The Wycliffe Bible Translators, Inc. is an organization founded in 1942 that has been translating the Bible into more and more languages every day.[38] The day is soon coming when every person on earth will have heard of Jesus, even if they do not accept Him as their Lord.

Michael L. Brown shows the exponential increase in translations in his discussion of the coming end of the Messianic (or Church) Age: "By the year 100 C.E., the Bible had been translated into only a handful of languages—fewer than six. By 200 C.E....the number had grown to seven. By the year 500, it had increased to thirteen, and by 1000 C.E., to just seventeen...By 1500 C.E., (translations had)...grown to 34,...and by 1800, to 67 translations....By 1900 the number had swelled to 537. By 2000, it was over 2000 translations.(some paraphrasing used by the author)."[39]   One can go on line to the Wycliffe website (see footnote) and actually see how many more languages are awaiting translation on any particular day.

---

[38] www.wycliffe.org

[39] <u>Answering Jewish Objections to Jesus, Vol. 1</u>, Michael L. Brown, Baker Books, 2000; pp. 91-92

This is one of the qualifying conditions set out in the Bible to alert those who seek to understand that the End Times have arrived. With television, easy travel, and dedicated missionaries, the Gospel can be broadcast or carried to every corner of the earth.

Some of the difficulty in taking the Gospel to the peoples of the world now centers around the governmental restraints on Christian missionary work. Most Muslim-controlled governments will not allow this. Certainly those governments controlled by Sharia law will not allow it. Also, certain Communist countries such as North Korea will not allow Christian missionaries into their country. Other Communist countries such as China, Vietnam, and Myanmar are allowing some Christian activity, but it is strictly controlled and limited.

# Fig Leaf #11:
# Abomination of Desolation

*"Therefore when you see the Abomination of Desolation which was spoken of through Daniel the prophet, standing in the holy place* (let the reader understand), *then those who are in Judea must flee to the mountains."* Matthew 24:15-16

Jesus then discussed the Abomination of Desolation described in Daniel.[40] He was referring to the Anti-Christ's standing in the Tribulation temple and declaring himself "god."[41] This event will occur in the middle of the seven-year Tribulation, at which time the Anti-Christ will declare the World Church illegal. He will demand that everyone worship him, and will place his statue in the Jewish Temple at that

---

[40] The Bible, through many authors; *"...therefore he will be disheartened and will return and become enraged at the holy covenant and take action; so he will come back and show regard for those who forsake the holy covenant. Forces from him will arise, desecrate the sanctuary fortress, and do away with the regular sacrifice. And they will set up the abomination of desolation."* Daniel 11:30-31 *"And he will make a firm covenant with the many for one week, but in the middle of the week he will put a stop to sacrifice and grain offering; and on the wing of abominations will come one who makes desolate, even until a complete destruction..."* Daniel 9:27.

[41] Regarding the Anti-Christ himself, *"There was given to him a mouth speaking arrogant words and blasphemies...and he opened his mouth in blasphemies against God, to blaspheme His name and His tabernacle...all who dwell on the earth will worship him..."* Revelation 13:5,6,8 (partial quotations). And regarding the "Prophet" who follows the Anti-Christ, *"He performs great signs, so that he even makes fire come down out of heaven to the earth in the presence of men. And he deceives those who dwell on the earth because of the signs which it was given him to perform in the presence of the beast, telling those who dwell on the earth to make an image to the beast who had the wound of the sword and has come to life. And it was given to him to give breath to the image of the beast, so that the image of the beast would even speak and cause as many as do not worship the image of the beast to be killed."* Revelation 13:13-15 *"...and the man of lawlessness is revealed, the son of destruction, who opposes and exalts himself above every so-called god or object of worship, so **that he takes his seat in the temple of God, displaying himself as being God**"* 2 Thessalonians 2:3b-4

time. He will begin to persecute the Jews, reneging on his peace accord with Israel that he had confirmed about 3 ½ years previously.

Many in the evangelical church believe that the Rapture will occur before this and that the Church will not be on earth to see this "fig leaf." However, this is not the interpretation of everyone in the church. Nonetheless, if for any reason, someone is still here when the Abomination occurs, he/she should understand that it is one of the signs described by Jesus. Once the Abomination has taken place, God's severe judgments known as the Trumpet and Bowl judgments (Revelation) will begin to wreak havoc on earth.

The original Abomination of Desolation occurred 180-190 years before Jesus spoke of this happening as a sign of His future coming. The original occurrence was in 167 B.C. when Antiochus Epiphanes defiled the Holy of Holies in Jerusalem. Antiochus Epiphanes is recognized as the "Type" or foreshadowing of the Final Anti-Christ.

The fact that Jesus spoke of this recurring in the future shows the foreshadowing aspect of this prophecy. Although the "type" occurred in 167 B.C., the "anti-type" or fulfillment will occur in the Last Days during the Tribulation.

# Fig Leaf #12:

# The Great Tribulation

*"For then there will be a great tribulation, such as has not occurred since the beginning of the world until now, nor ever will. Unless those days had been cut short, no life would have been saved; but for the sake of the elect those days will be cut short. Then if anyone says to you, 'Behold, here is the Christ,' or 'There He is,' do not believe him. For false christs and false prophets will arise and will show great signs and wonders, so as to mislead, if possible, even the elect. Behold, I have told you in advance."*
Matthew 24: 21-25

Next Jesus stated that there will be a Great Tribulation of such intensity that the world will have never seen anything like it previously, nor will people ever see anything like it afterwards. It will be a three and a half year period during which the awesome and terrible judgments of God are poured out on the earth. Jesus told his disciples that the days of the Tribulation will have to be shortened in order for any of the saints to survive. He noted that false christs and false prophets will arise who mislead many through great signs and wonders.

The Tribulation is divided into two sections: the first 3 ½ years before the Abomination of Desolation and the final 3 ½ years of the "Great Tribulation." In the first period before the Abomination occurs, the Anti-Christ will become established and his prophet will set up the World Religion. Multitudes of people around the world will recognize the "signs of the time" and will decide to follow the Lord. It will be a difficult time for them, and many will be killed by the governing regime. This will be the time that the Seven Seals will be opened in Heaven by Jesus (Revelation, chapters 6 and 7).

During the first 3 ½ years, the Two Witnesses will prophecy in Jerusalem (Revelation 11:3-11). Their ministry will last 3 ½ years and may or may not overlap into the final Great Tribulation. Throughout the seven years of the Tribulation, the 144,000 Jewish evangelists will continue to bring multitudes of people to the saving knowledge of who Jesus is and how His sacrifice has redeemed them from God's wrath (Revelation 7:4-8).

After the Abomination is set up in the Temple in Jerusalem, God's final and most severe judgments begin. First are the seven Trumpet judgments which afflict a third of the world each time (Revelation 8:6-13; 9:1-21; 11:15-19). Following the Trumpet judgments, the terrible seven Bowl judgments are released. These are the most severe and afflict the entire earth (Revelation 16:1-12, 17-21).

The terrible Day of the Lord begins after the devastation of the Trumpet and Bowl judgments are completed.

# Fig Leaf #13:

## The Day of the Lord

*"But immediately after the tribulation of those days the sun will be darkened, and the moon will not give its light, and the stars will fall from the sky, and the powers of the heavens will be shaken."* <u>Matthew 24:29</u>

Toward the end of the Great Tribulation, the sun will darken, the moon will not give light, and the powers of heaven will be shaken. These are the Great Signs in the Heavens spoken of by Jesus. These signs will occur late in the tribulation and are associated with the "Day of the Lord."

The Day of the Lord is spoken of by the various prophets as a "terrible" day. It is not considered a 24 hour "day,' but rather a period of time during which the Lord's judgments and justice will be poured out on the earth and its inhabitants. The current era is a dispensation of God's love and mercy, but in the Day of the Lord, God's justice toward sin on earth will dominate.

The Bible warns us in the book of Hebrews that:
*"If we deliberately keep on sinning after we have received the knowledge of the truth, no sacrifice for sins is left, but only a fearful expectation of judgment and of raging fire that will consume the enemies of God. Anyone who rejected the law of Moses died without mercy on the testimony of two or three witnesses. How much more severely do you think someone deserves to be punished who has trampled the Son of God underfoot, who has treated as an unholy thing the blood of the covenant that sanctified them, and who has insulted the Spirit of grace? For we know him who said, "It is mine to avenge; I will repay," and again, "The Lord will judge his people." It is a*

*dreadful thing to fall into the hands of the living God.*"
<u>Hebrews 10:26-31</u>

For almost 2000 years, since the death of Jesus on the
cross, and the redemption made possible by His blood
sacrifice, mankind has had readily available mercy and grace
poured out on us. God has made every effort to bring as many
of His children as possible back into His fold. But once the
Tribulation begins, His mercy will be overshadowed by the
power of His judgment on those people who have rejected
Him. The Era of Mercy will be replaced by the Era of Justice.
God's vengeance will finally begin to fall on those who hate
and reject Him and who also hate His children.

The final sentence of the above quote from the book of
Hebrews should chill the soul of anyone who has fought
against God. It is indeed a terrifying thing to fall into the
hands of a just God without hope of mercy. No person's
"goodness" or good deeds will be sufficient to save them from
God's wrath toward sin. Only by accepting the redemption
offered by the sacrifice of Jesus can those sins we all have
deep in our souls be covered. Once we agree to turn away
from sin and accept that redemption bought for us by Jesus on
the cross, then our sins will be declared "Justified" and
remembered no more. From then on, if we continue to walk
with the Holy Spirit's guidance, we will no longer have to fear
the Justice and Judgment of God. No longer will we have to
worry about falling into the hands of the living God. We will
be observers, but not participants, in that final awful judgment.

# Fig Leaf #14:

# The Sign of the Lord &

# The Second Coming of Jesus

*"And then the sign of the Son of man will appear in the sky, and then all the tribes of the earth will mourn, and they will see the Son of Man coming on the clouds of the sky with power and great glory. And He will send forth His angels with a great trumpet and they will gather together His elect from the four winds, from one end of the sky to the other."* <u>Matthew 24:30-31</u>

Then the sign of the Lord will appear in the sky where everyone will see it, and the Lord will come with power and great glory. If someone is there when the Second Coming occurs and has still not discerned that Jesus is on His way back to earth, he probably has been in a coma or denial for seven years—or has been unaware of the Biblical teaching, or just rebellious against God and His Word. This sign is, of course, the final and ultimate sign of Yeshua's return and comes at the end of the Great Tribulation.

There has been much speculation regarding the Sign of the Son of Man. No one knows what that sign will be. But everyone on earth will be able to see it! Many have speculated that whatever it is, it will be broadcast around the world on television or the internet. Others have said that it will be an unprecedented supernatural occurrence that everyone will be able to see with their own eyes.

When Jesus comes back (the Second Coming), he will come on the clouds of the sky as prophesied in Daniel and repeated by the angels at His Ascension
*"In my vision at night I looked, and there before me was one like a son of man, coming with the clouds of heaven. He*

*approached the Ancient of Days and was led into his presence. He was given authority, glory and sovereign power; all nations and peoples of every language worshiped him. His dominion is an everlasting dominion that will not pass away, and his kingdom is one that will never be destroyed."* <u>Daniel 7:13-14</u>

*"After he said this, he was taken up before their very eyes, and a cloud hid him from their sight. They were looking intently up into the sky as he was going, when suddenly two men dressed in white stood beside them. "Men of Galilee," they said, "why do you stand here looking into the sky? This same Jesus, who has been taken from you into heaven, will come back in the same way you have seen him go into heaven."* <u>Acts 1:9-11</u>

Jesus will destroy the Anti-Christ and his prophet along with all of their armies. He will then establish the Millennial Kingdom.

# TABLE OF SIGNS

The signs or fig leaves as given by Jesus
Matthew 24, Mark 13 and Luke 17, 21

## Signs & Fulfillment:

**1.Nation vs. Nation; Kingdom vs. Kingdom**
   WWI (1914-1918) & WWII (1939-1945)
   Matthew 24: 7; Mark 13:8; Luke 21: 10
   (Fulfilled)

**2.Plagues**
   Flu Epidemic of 1918
   HIV (AIDS) 1982
   SARS 2003
   "Bird Flu" still looming
   Matthew 24: 7; Mark 13:8; Luke 21:11
   (Partially fulfilled)

**3.Earthquakes**
   Intensity and Frequency increasing
   Matthew 24:7; Mark 13:8; Luke 21:12
   (Partially Fulfilled)

**4.Famines**
   Russia, China, Biafra
   Matthew 24:7; Mark 13:8; Luke 21:12
   (Partially Fulfilled)

**5.Hatred of Christians**
   Christians characterized as old-fashioned,
   small-minded, judgmental, & backward:
   Considered obstructionists to New World Order
   Matthew 24:9
   (Partially Fulfilled)

## 6.Apostasy

Wellhausen (Documentary Hypothesis)1899
Weiss, Holtzmann, Gunkel  Pre-WWI
Gunkel, Bultmann (Form Criticism)  1941
Albertz, Dibelius, Schmidt,  Humanistic Christology
Altizer,Vahanian, van Buren  "God Is Dead" 1960s
Jesus Seminar 1990s
Episcopal Bishop Spong (Believer in Exile) 1990s
Matthew 24:10; 1 Timothy4:1-5; Daniel 12:10
2 Peter 2:1; Acts 20: 29-30; 2 Timothy 4:3-4
(Partially Fulfilled)

## 7.Deception

False prophets, false christs.  Decrease in personal integrity
Jim Jones 1978;
David Koresh and Branch Davidians 1993
Heaven's Gate 1997
Matthew 24:5,11,24; 2 Timothy 3:13
(Partially Fulfilled)

## 8.Lawlessness

Increase in Crime
Disregard for Rules of Civility
Matthew 24:12; 2 Timothy 3:3-4; Jude 8
(Partially Fulfilled)

## 9.Loss of Love

Fear to help others; Hardening of Hearts
Matthew 24:12; 2 Timothy 3:3
(Partially Fulfilled)

## 10.Gospel Preached in the Whole World

Wycliffe Bible Translators
Increased transportation and communications
Matthew 24:14; Mark 13:10
(Partially Fulfilled)

**11.Abomination of Desolation**
  Midway through the Tribulation
  Matthew 24:15; Mark 13:14
  (Unfulfilled)

**12.Great Tribulation**
  Trumpet and Bowl Judgments
  Matthew 24:21; Mark 13:19
  (Unfulfilled)

**13.Great Signs in the Heavens**
  Sun and Moon will not shine
  Matthew 24:29; Mark 13:24, 25; Luke 21:25
  (Unfulfilled)

**14.The Sign In the Sky/Second Coming**
  Jesus is Coming!
  Matthew 24:30; Mark 13:26; Luke 21:27
  (Unfulfilled)

The above list is the overview of the signs and wonders and events (the fig leaves) that will come upon the Earth in the End Times.

# CHAPTER 5

# Prophecies
# Concerning Israel

When God promised the Holy Land to Abraham, He specifically proclaimed a blessing and a curse for everyone else regarding His Chosen People.

*"Go from your country, your people and your father's household to the land I will show you.* *"I will make you into a great nation, and I will bless you; I will make your name great, and you will be a blessing,* **I will bless those who bless you, and whoever curses you I will curse;** *and all peoples on earth will be blessed through you."* <u>Genesis 12:1-3</u>.

This promise of God's involves every nation on earth, and ties them to the descendants of Abraham in a very real and palpable manner. We are called to pray for Israel, and for God's blessing on that land and country, and in doing so, we will be blessed. The fall of the U.S. from superpower status will no doubt be tied to the government's reversal of American support for Israel.

The prophecies regarding Israel are important in discerning if we are in the End Times. We know that as the world descends into the Tribulation, that all world events will begin to focus on Israel. The U.S. and Europe will become secondary entities, and may not survive as independent nations as the One World movement becomes stronger. But Israel will survive, and will become the center of the secular world's attention.

*"A prophecy: The word of the LORD concerning Israel. The LORD, who stretches out the heavens, who lays the foundation of the earth, and who forms the human spirit within a person, declares: "I am going to make Jerusalem a cup that sends all the surrounding peoples reeling. Judah will be besieged as well as Jerusalem. On that day, when all the nations of the earth are gathered against her, **I will make Jerusalem an immovable rock for all the nations. All who try to move it will injure themselves.**"* Zechariah 12: 1-3

There will be much negative propaganda and striving against the Lord's people—the Jews—and His holy city, Jerusalem. We are seeing this being fulfilled. The United Nations has become the main supporter and ally of the Palestinian Authority, and their fight against the country of Israel. Jerusalem is the center of attention from the U.N. and the humanist world. The world news organizations repeatedly frame Israel as an oppressive nation, in spite of the reality of a people fighting to defend themselves against an enemy that has sworn to wipe them off of the face of the earth. Humanists all over the world are joining the anti-Semitic DBS (Divest, Boycott, and Sanction) movement against Israel.

The U.N. will continue to accept the perverted idea that Jerusalem is a Muslim holy site, and that there never was a Jewish temple in that city in past ages. As the world nurtures the altered history put forth by the Muslims, and continue to badger Israel, the tension in Jerusalem and Israel will continue to increase. But why Jerusalem? Why not any other city in the world?  Read the prophecy above in Zechariah again.  This must happen so that God's plan regarding the Last Days are accomplished.

# PROPHECIES FROM EZEKIEL,
# JEREMIAH, AND ISAIAH

The prophet Ezekiel was given visions and oracles from God while the Jews were in captivity in Babylon. It is thought that he was taken captive to Babylon in 597 B.C., in the second wave of captivity. While he was in captivity, Jerusalem was destroyed by Babylon in 586 B.C. He was called by God as a prophet in 593 B.C. and ended his prophetic ministry in 571 B.C. The prophet Isaiah lived over a hundred years before Ezekiel. He began his ministry in 740 B.C. and prophesied under the reigns of at least four kings: Uzziah, Jotham, Ahaz, and Hezekiah.

He prophesied about the destruction of the earth and the deliverance of Israel, as described in chapters 24-27 of his book of prophecy, which are known as the Apocalypse of Isaiah. He foresaw the rise and fall of Babylon, even though the world power in his day was Assyria, and Babylon was just another vassal state. He foresaw and named Cyrus as the future ruler who would release the Jewish captives. (Isaiah was a prophet from 740 to 681 B.C. Cyrus ruled the Medo-Persian empire from 559-530 B.C. and allowed the Jewish captives to return to Jerusalem starting in 538 B.C.) Isaiah also foresaw the creation of a new heaven and earth and the Peaceful Kingdom (Chapters 65-66).

There are five major prophecies from the book of Ezekiel that we will consider here. Two major prophecies from Isaiah may have relevance to this discussion, even though they will probably be fulfilled during the late Tribulation and the Millennial Kingdom. Multiple other prophecies from Isaiah support the visions of Ezekiel and John (Revelations). These are major prophecies which are being fulfilled.

# Fig Leaf #15:

# Israel Restored

God revealed that Israel would be restored. This prophecy was fulfilled twice; the first time with the return from the Babylonian exile in 538 B.C., and this second and last time from 1917 to 1948. Since Israel declared itself to be a nation in 1948, the numbers of Jews moving to Israel (making aliyah) has continued to increase each year. The following Biblical verses illustrate the numerous times that God declares His intention to bring His chosen people back into the land He promised them through the Patriarchs.

God, through his prophet Ezekiel, expressed His intent to personally bring His People out of the "lands where you are scattered" and "bring you into the land of Israel." (Note: He did not say He would bring them into the land of "Palestine.)"

"' As surely as I live, declares the Sovereign LORD, I will reign over you with a mighty hand and an outstretched arm and with outpoured wrath. I will bring you from the nations and gather you from the countries where you have been scattered ... Then you will know that I am the LORD, when I bring you into the land of Israel, the land I had sworn with uplifted hand to give to your ancestors.'" Ezekiel 20: 33-34,42[42]

---

[42] The Bible, God through many authors: "...with a mighty hand and with an outstretched arm and with wrath poured out; and I will bring you into the wilderness of the peoples, and there I will enter into judgment with you face to face. ...For on My holy mountain, on the high mountain of Israel,' declares the Lord God, 'there the whole house of Israel, all of them, will serve Me in the land; there I will accept them and there I will seek your contributions and the choicest of your gifts, with all your holy things. As a soothing aroma I will accept you when I bring you out from the peoples and gather you from the lands where you are scattered; and I will prove Myself holy among you in the sight of the nations. And you will know that I am the Lord, when I bring you into the

*"Thus says the Lord God, 'When I gather the house of Israel from the peoples among whom they are scattered, and will manifest My holiness in them in the sight of the nations, then they will live in their land which I gave to My servant Jacob.* They will live in it securely; and they will build houses, plant vineyards and live securely when I execute judgments upon all who scorn them round about them. Then they will know that I am the Lord their God.'"* <u>Ezekiel 28: 25-26</u>

God has stated that He will bring His people out of the nations (the dispersion of Jews throughout the nations is known as the Diaspora) and will re-establish them in the Holy Land, now called Israel again. God has stated that He will bring His people into the *"land of Israel, into the land which I swore to give to your forefathers."* And again, *"they will live in their land which I gave to My servant Jacob."* There has been a strong movement over the past few years to call the Holy Land by the name of "Palestine". There have even been Christians who state that history supports the name "Palestine" over the name "Israel". The verses above clearly call the land, "Israel", and God clearly states that He has given that land to His people, the Jews. The anti-Semitic Roman ruler, Hadrian, renamed the land, calling it "Palestine" (actually Syria Palaistina) after his legions put down the Jewish uprising in 135 A.D. (C.E.) led by Bar Kochba. He drove the Jews out of the area called Judea, razed Jerusalem, and built a new city which he renamed Aeolia Capitolina. Incidentally, Hadrian also hated Christians.

When Constantine became emperor of Rome in 306 C.E. and allowed Christianity to be openly practiced within the Empire, his mother, Queen Helena, made a pilgrimage to the city now called Jerusalem again and identified the holy sites, building churches over them. The area was known as Palestine by people in the West, but locals considered themselves Syrians. The name, Palestine, would emerge again

---

*land of Israel, into the land which I swore to give to your forefathers.'"*
<u>Ezekiel 20: 34b-35,40-42</u>

after the British took control after World War I. Prior to then, the area was considered a part of Syria, and the nomadic residents considered themselves Syrian Arabs. Today, non-Jewish residents of Israel call themselves Palestinians, and try to trace their families back to the Philistines of ancient times. The history of the area would instead say that they were not called Palestinians until the British mandate in 1917. The verses above show the truth that God called the area "Israel" 2600 years ago.

Now that the country of Israel has been miraculously born, and strengthened primarily through the efforts of the United States, we know through prophecy that there will be several times of trials coming upon them.

Today, in the early twenty-first century, the prophetic verses of Psalm 83 jump out at us:

> *"O God, do not remain quiet:*
> *Do not be silent and, O God, do not be still.*
> *For behold, Your enemies make an uproar,*
> *And those who hate You have exalted themselves.*
> *They make shrewd plans against your people*
> *And conspire together against Your treasured ones.*
> *They have said, 'Come, and let us wipe them out as a nation,*
> *That the name of Israel be remembered no more.'*
> *For they have conspired together with one mind;*
> *Against You they make a covenant."* <u>Psalm 83: 1-5</u>

The psalmist then names the ancient nations that surround Israel as the ones who are trying to "wipe them out as a nation." Edomites and Ishmaelites were descendants of Esau and Ishmael, and lived east of the Dead Sea in what is today southern Jordan and northwest Saudi Arabia. Ammonites and Moabites were the descendants of Lot, and lived in what is today northern Jordan and southern Syria.

The people of Philistia and Tyre would have lived in today's Lebanon. Assyria is today's Syria and Iraq.

But there are even more stressful times coming upon Israel in the near future. Ezekiel tells us about a planned invasion by the hordes of Gog and Magog, which is discussed later. The prophet Jeremiah relates a time even after then:

> *"Alas! For that day is great,*
> *There is none like it;*
> *And it is the time of Jacob's distress,*
> *But he will be saved from it."* Jeremiah 30:7

This will occur during the Tribulation after the Abomination of Desolation takes place. Jerusalem and Israel will become the center of the wars that rage between the Anti-Christ and his political enemies, and much destruction will occur until the Second Coming of Jesus halts the war. Jesus will then establish His Millennial Kingdom centered in Israel.

The following verses speak of the Davidic Kingdom, also known as the Millennial Kingdom. God again promises to restore His people to their Land.

> *"For this is what the Sovereign LORD says:* ***I myself will*** *search for my sheep and look after them ....*
> ***I will bring them out from the nations and gather them*** *from the countries, and* ***I will bring them into their own land;*** *I will pasture them on* ***the mountains of Israel,*** *in the ravines and in all the settlements in the land.*
> ***I will place over them one shepherd, my servant David,*** *and he will tend them; he will tend them and be their shepherd.* ***I the LORD will be their God, and my servant David will be*** *prince among them. I the LORD have spoken.*
> *They will know that I am the LORD, when I break the bars of their yoke and rescue them from the hands of those who enslaved them.* ***They will no longer be plundered by the nations,***

*nor will wild animals devour them; They will live in safety, and*
*no one will make them afraid.*

*Then they will know that I, the LORD their God, am with*
*them and that they, the Israelites, are my people, declares the*
*Sovereign LORD." Ezekiel 34: 11,13, 23,27b,28,30*[43]

God promises to provide His People with a land that
He will bless and make secure. The People were dispersed,
and God Himself manipulated events so that they would come
back to the land He has given them. He will continue to
provide Divine protection over them as a people.

God then states that He will not only bless His people,
but also the Holy Land itself once the Jews return to it.

*"But you, O mountains of Israel, you will put forth your*
*branches and bear your fruit for My people Israel; for they will*
*soon come.*

*For, behold, I am for you, and I will turn to you, and you*
*will be cultivated and sown. **I will multiply men on you, all the***

---

[43] The Bible, God through many authors: " *I will feed My flock and I will*
*lead them to rest,' declares the Lord God. 'I will seek the lost, bring back the*
*scattered, bind up the broken and strengthen the sick;...therefore, I will deliver*
*My flock, and they will no longer be a prey; and I will judge between one sheep*
*and another.* **Then I will set over them one shepherd, My servant David, and**
**he will feed them; he will feed them himself and be their shepherd. And I, the**
**Lord, will be their God, and My servant David sill be prince among them**; *I the*
*Lord have spoken. I will make a covenant of peace with them and eliminate*
*harmful beasts from the land so that they may live securely in the wilderness and*
*sleep in the woods.* **I will make them and the places around My hill a blessing.**
*And I will cause showers to come down in their season; they will be showers of*
*blessing. Also the tree of the field will yield its fruit and the earth will yield its*
*increase, and they will be secure on their land. Then they will know that I am the*
*Lord, when I have broken the bars of their yoke and have delivered them from*
*the hand of those who enslaved them.* **They will no longer be a prey to the**
**nations, and the beasts of the earth will not devour them; but they will live**
**securely, and no one will make them afraid.** *I will establish for them a*
*renowned planting place, and they will not again be victims of famine in the land,*
*and they will not endure the insults of the nations anymore. Then they will know*
*that I, the Lord their God, am with them, and that they, the house of Israel, are*
*My people,' declares the Lord God. 'As for you, My sheep, the sheep of My*
*pasture, you are men, and I am your God,' declares the Lord God.* Ezekiel 34:
15-16, 22-31

*house of Israel, all of it; and the cities will be inhabited and the waste places will be rebuilt.*

*I will multiply on you man and beast; and they will increase and be fruitful; and I will cause you to be inhabited as you were formerly and will treat you better than at the first. Thus you will know that I am the Lord.*

*Yes, I will cause men—My people Israel—to walk on you and possess you, so that you will become their inheritance and never again bereave them of children."* <u>Ezekiel 36: 8-12</u>

God's promise to revitalize the Holy Land when His people are returned has been realized. Israel is now an exporter of fruits and foodstuffs. Also the green vegetation of the parts of Israel controlled by the Jewish state stand in harsh contrast to the bleak parts of Israel now controlled by the "Palestinians." If one drives from Tel Aviv on the coast directly to Bethlehem, one would leave the forested hills and lush valleys of the Jewish area, and pass into the sparsely vegetated countryside of the Palestinian Authority. Again, God's prophecies from Ezekiel are being fulfilled now.

God also gave an explanation for His zeal to bring the children of Jacob back into the land of Israel.

*"Therefore say to the Israelites, 'This is what the Sovereign LORD says: It is not for your sake, people of Israel, that I am going to do these things, but for the sake of my holy name, which you have profaned among the nations where you have gone.*

*I will show the holiness of My great name, which has been profaned among the nations, the name you have profaned among them.*

*Then the nations will know that I am the LORD, declares the Sovereign LORD, when I am proved holy through you before their eyes*

*'For I will take you out of the nations; I will gather you from all the countries and bring you back into your own land."* <u>Ezekiel 36: 22-24</u>

94

In this day of general revolt against God among the peoples of the world, God has promised that the re-formation of the nation of Israel is a sign to all of the world that God is who He says He is. Not only is He real, but He is still in control of this world!

We have discussed God's plan for His People as revealed in four chapters of Ezekiel so far. However, the most explicit prophecy comes from the 37th chapter of Ezekiel.

This chapter of Ezekiel reveals the clearest picture of God's plan to restore His people, the Jews, onto the land that He promised their ancestors. This is the most significant and revealing "Fig Leaf" we have before us today. For that reason, most of the chapter will be quoted here.

*"The hand of the LORD was on me, and he brought me out by the Spirit of the LORD and set me in the middle of a valley; it was full of bones. He led me back and forth among them, and I saw a great many bones on the floor of the valley, bones that were very dry. He asked me, "Son of man, can these bones live?"*

*I said, "Sovereign LORD, you alone know." Then he said to me, "Prophesy to these bones and say to them, 'Dry bones, hear the word of the LORD!* **This is what the Sovereign LORD says to these bones: I will make breath enter you, and you will come to life. I will attach tendons to you and make flesh come upon you and cover you with skin; I will put breath in you, and you will come to life. Then you will know that I am the LORD.'"**

*So I prophesied as I was commanded. And as I was prophesying, there was a noise, a rattling sound, and the bones came together, bone to bone. I looked, and tendons and flesh appeared on them and skin covered them, but there was no breath in them. Then he said to me, "Prophesy to the breath; prophesy, son of man, and say to it, 'This is what the Sovereign LORD says: Come, breath, from the four winds and breathe into these slain, that they may live.'*

**So I prophesied as he commanded me, and breath entered them; they came to life and stood up on their feet—a**

**vast army.** *Then he said to me: "Son of man, these bones are the people of Israel. They say, 'Our bones are dried up and our hope is gone; we are cut off.' Therefore prophesy and say to them: 'This is what the Sovereign LORD says:* **My people, I am going to open your graves and bring you up from them; I will bring you back to the land of Israel.** *Then you, my people, will know that I am the LORD, when I open your graves and bring you up from them.* **I will put my Spirit in you and you will live, and I will settle you in your own land.** *Then you will know that I the LORD have spoken, and I have done it, declares the LORD.'"* <u>Ezekiel 37:1-14</u>

*"And say to them, 'This is what the Sovereign LORD says:* **I will take the Israelites out of the nations where they have gone. I will gather them from all around and bring them back into their own land. I will make them one nation in the land, on the mountains of Israel**

*...They will be my people, and I will be their God."* **'My servant David will be king over them, and they will all have one shepherd. They will follow my laws and be careful to keep my decrees. They will live in the land I gave to my servant Jacob, the land where your ancestors lived. They and their children and their children's children will live there forever, and David my servant will be their prince forever.**

*I will make a covenant of peace with them; it will be an everlasting covenant. I will establish them and increase their numbers, and I will put my sanctuary among them forever. My dwelling place will be with them; I will be their God, and they will be my people. Then the nations will know that I the LORD make Israel holy, when my sanctuary is among them forever.'"* <u>Ezekiel 37: 21-28</u>

God was clearly communicating through Ezekiel that He would take the "bones" or remnants of the Jews, and put them back together with "muscle" and "flesh" and "skin" to make a complete nation.

Has this not happened over the past century just as God said?  The Zionist movement began in the late 1800s just in time to gather momentum by World War I.  The land now called Israel, a neglected backwater part of the Ottoman Empire by that time, was turned over to the British to administer after the war.  The British government issued the Balfour Declaration supporting a Jewish homeland in the area then called Palestine.  Jews from all around the world began moving into the area, as did Arabs from the surrounding lands.  As the two populations grew, hostilities broke out, making the governance of the area very uncomfortable for the British.  They called for the original "Two Nation" solution, calling for the land west of the Jordan River to be a homeland for Jews (but Arabs were also welcome).  They established the Kingdom of Jordan east of the river, but Jews were not welcome to move there.  By the end of World War II, the U.N. became the mediator of the area and approved the Two Nation solution.  The new nation of Israel, established in 1948 had to immediately fight for its life against the well-trained and well-equipped armies of five Arab nations.  Despite the odds of defeating such a large army, the poorly equipped Israelis did just that.  The Hand of God was clearly involved in the establishment of Israel.

God also declares not only His intentions to gather His people back to the Holy Land, but also His intentions that when this happens, the Jews and the world will understand Who God is.  He states that He will be revealed to everyone in the world.

*"Therefore this is what the Sovereign LORD says: I will now restore the fortunes of Jacob and will have compassion on all the people of Israel, and I will be zealous for my holy name. They will forget their shame and all the unfaithfulness they showed toward me when they lived in safety in their land with no one to make them afraid.*

**When I have brought them back from the nations and**

97

*have gathered them from the countries of their enemies, I will*
*be proved holy through them in the sight of many nations.* Then
*they will know that I am the LORD their God, for though I sent*
*them into exile among the nations,* **I will gather them to their**
**own land, not leaving any behind. I will no longer hide my face**
**from them, for I will pour out my Spirit on the people of Israel,**
*declares the Sovereign LORD."* Ezekiel 39: 25-29

Jeremiah also saw the restoration of Israel. Although
he was possibly thinking of the return of the Jews from
Babylon, the last verses suggest that the Babylonian
restoration was a type for the future events.

> *"Thus says the Lord,*
> *'Behold, I will restore the fortunes of the tents of Jacob*
> *And have compassion on his dwelling places;*
> *And I will multiply them and they will not be diminished;*
> *I will also honor them and they will not be insignificant.*
> *And their congregation shall be established before Me;*
> *And I will punish all their oppressors.*
> *You shall be My people, And I will be your God.'"*
> *Behold, the tempest of the Lord!*
> *Wrath has gone forth, A sweeping tempest;*
> *It will burst on the head of the wicked.*
> *The fierce anger of the Lord will not turn back*
> *Until He has performed and until He has accomplished*
> *The intent of His heart;*
> *In the latter days you will understand this.* Jeremiah
> 30:18,19b,20b,22-24

The prophets Isaiah, Amos, and Obadiah also saw the
restoration promised by God.

*"I will bring forth descendants from Jacob, and from*
*Judah those who will possess my mountains;* **my chosen people**
**will inherit them, and there will my servants live."** Isaiah 65: 9

*"And I will bring my people Israel back from exile. They will rebuild the ruined cities and live in them. They will plant vineyards and drink their wine; they will make gardens and eat their fruit. **I will plant Israel in their own land, never again to be uprooted from the land I have given them,**" says the LORD your God.* Amos 9:14-15

*"But on Mount Zion will be deliverance, and it will be holy, **and the house of Jacob will possess its inheritance.** Obadiah 17*[44]

The number of passages devoted by God in assuring His people that He would restore them to the land He promised to Abraham emphasizes how great of a priority this is for God.

In the passages noted above, God promised restoration of Israel not just somewhere in the world, but in their Middle Eastern homeland. The clearest prophecy is the 37th chapter of Ezekiel quoted above. God showed Ezekiel a valley full of dried human bones. As Ezekiel watched, the bones came together with a noise, and were covered with muscle and flesh. And then they came to life and stood on their feet, as Ezekiel said, "an exceedingly great army." This is the illustration God used to show how Israel would be restored as a nation. God described the dried bones as the dried up hopes of Jews around the world. He promised that He would open up their "graves" and bring them into the land of Israel.

---

[44] The Bible, God through many authors: *"But on Mount Zion will be deliverance, and it will be holy, **and the house of Jacob will possess its inheritance. ...** Then those of the Negev* [the barren wilderness of southern Judah] *will possess the mountains of Esau, and those of the Shephelah* [the foothills of western Judah] *the Philistine plain; they will occupy the fields of Ephraim and Samaria, and Benjamin will possess Gilead. And the exiles of this host of the sons of Israel, who are among the Canaanites as far as Zarephath, and the exiles of Jerusalem who are in Sepharad will possess the cities of the Negev. The deliverers will ascend Mount Zion to judge the mountain of Esau, and the kingdom will be the Lord's."* Obadiah 17, 19-21

While this may yet be literally fulfilled at the time of the Millennial Kingdom, it has been figuratively fulfilled during the 20<sup>th</sup> Century. The "graves" that held the dried bones were figuratively those countries which oppressed and denigrated the Jews. Obviously, the oppression and horrors imposed on the Jews by Hitler and Stalin could be seen as graves for the hopes of the Jews. However, after WWII, these countries were opened up, and Jews were allowed and encouraged to leave. But where could they go? Many elected to go to the new country of Israel. The Jews who had been able to get out of Europe and Russia before the war continued to look for a permanent home, since they would not be welcomed back in their previous homes.

During the early twentieth century, with the destruction of the Ottoman Empire, and especially after Israel was established as a country, Jews from all around the Mediterranean and other areas such as Russia, began to flow into the new country. Jews have continued to pour into the land promised to Abraham by God.

The Promised Land that He opened up for them after the death of Moses, under the command of Joshua, would be their land forever. God would restore them twice as noted above. The first restoration would be at the end of their captivity in Babylon. But the final restoration would come at a later time. That time was 1948.

The prophecy of Isaiah 11:11 states:
*"Then it will happen on that day that the Lord will again recover the second time with His hand the remnant of His people, who will remain, from Assyria, Egypt, Pathros, Cush, Elam, Shinar, Hamath, and from the islands of the sea."*

His Word clearly says that He would bring them back to the Holy Land not once, but twice.

Also, look at verses 10 and 12 of Isaiah 11:

*"In that day, the **Root of Jesse will stand as a banner for the peoples...He will raise a banner for the nations and gather the exiles of Israel; He will assemble the scattered people of Judah from the four quarters of the earth.**"*

It is not a random happening that the young nation of Israel picked the Star of David, (Jesse's son) as the center of their national flag! This flag, carrying the emblem of David, from whom comes Yeshua, the Root of Jesse, does indeed stand over the land where God has once again (the second time) gathered the exiles of Israel.

Although we say that this prophecy of restoring Israel has been fulfilled—but part of it actually has not.

Look at Ezekiel 36: 26-27 *"I will give you a new heart and put a new spirit in you; I will remove from you your heart of stone and give you a heart of flesh. And **I will put My Spirit in you** and move you to follow My decrees and be careful to keep My laws"*.

This part about God pouring His Spirit on the Jews is considered unfulfilled. Many think this will occur during the Tribulation, but certainly before the Millennium.

The following timeline shows events in the past that establish the children of Israel as the "owners" of the land of Israel. It also reveals the historical events that merged to form the Nation of Israel.

# The Timeline of Events of Israel

<u>1400-1300 BC</u>:  The children of Israel conquered Canaan under Joshua.

<u>1000 BC</u>:  King David's Kingdom

<u>930 BC</u>:  King Solomon died and the Kingdom was split into two parts: Israel in the north with 10 tribes, and Judah in the south with the tribes of Judah and Benjamin.

<u>722 BC</u>:  The northern kingdom, Israel, was destroyed by Assyria and the 10 tribes carried into captivity.

<u>612 BC</u>:  The Assyrian capital of Ninevah destroyed by Babylon

<u>609 BC</u>:  Pharaoh Neco of Egypt joined the Assyrians against the Babylonians at Carchemish (now in southern Turkey)

<u>609 BC</u>: King Josiah of Judah attempted to stop Pharaoh Neco at Meggido and was killed

<u>609 BC</u>: Pharaoh Neco set up Josiah's son, Jehoikim as a vassal king of Judah subject to Egypt

<u>605 BC</u>:  Nebuchadnezzar, king of Babylon, destroyed the Assyrians and routed the Egyptians at the battle of Carchemish

<u>605 BC</u>:  The Babylonians took King Jehoikim and the Judean leaders into captivity; this was the <u>First Wave of Captivity</u> and included Daniel, Hananiah (Shadrach), Mishael (Meshach), and Azariah (Abednego).  King Jehoikim was allowed to return to Jerusalem later.

<u>597 BC</u>: Jehoikim rebelled against Babylon, switching his allegiance to Egypt.  He died and was replaced by his son, Jehoikin.  The Babylonians again invaded and took King Jehoikin to Babylon and replaced him with his uncle,

Zedekiah. 10,000 Judeans, including Ezekiel, were taken captive to Babylon. This was the <u>Second Wave of Captivity</u>.

**588-586 BC**: Zedekiah rebelled against Babylon and Jerusalem was under siege by the Babylonian army. The city was completely destroyed, including the temple, and all the people were taken to Babylon in captivity. This was the <u>Third (and final) Wave of Captivity</u>.

<u>586 BC</u>: Judah was destroyed by Babylon and the 2 tribes of Judah and Benjamin carried into captivity

<u>538 BC</u>: Cyrus allowed some Jews to return to Jerusalem and rebuild the temple

<u>515 BC</u>: The Second Temple was completed

<u>445 BC</u>: The walls of Jerusalem were rebuilt

<u>333 BC</u>:  Alexander the Great began his conquests and conquered the Persian Empire, including Egypt

<u>323 BC</u>:  Alexander died and his kingdom was divided into 4 parts, under the control of 4 of his generals: Syria and Persia under Seleucus, Egypt under Ptolemy, Asia Minor under Lysimachus, and Macedonia and Greece under Antipater

<u>252-167 BC</u>: Seleucid Wars between the Syrian (Seleucid) and Egyptian (Ptolemaic) dynasties (these were Greek dynasties over these areas as above)

<u>201 BC</u>:  End of the Second Punic War established Rome as a new power in the Mediterranean area

<u>192 BC</u>:  Rome defeated the Seleucid army of Antiochus in Greece and drove them back into Asia Minor and again defeated them at the battle of Magnesia: Rome was then the most powerful nation of the Mediterranean

167 BC:  The Seleucid king, Antiochus Epiphanes desecrated the temple by sacrificing a pig on the altar

165 BC:  Maccabean Revolt.  Mattathias and his five sons began to throw off the Greek reign over the Holy Land.  The revolt was led by his son, Judas Maccabee (the hammer)

164 BC:  The temple was re-consecrated by Judas and the Festival of Hanukkah (Lights) established

164 BC:  Judas Maccabee became the High Priest and the Hasmonian Dynasty began; Judas negotiated a treaty with Rome

65 BC: Rome began expansion of its conquests into Asia

63 BC:  The Roman general Pompey conquered Jerusalem and entered the Holy of Holies

44 BC:  Julius Caesar was murdered.

44-40 BC:  Roman civil war, and Herod, general of the Hasmonian army allied first with Marc Antony, and subsequently with Octavius, later known as Caesar Augustus

40 BC:  Herod was named King over Israel by the Romans and essentially ended the Hasmonian dynasty

3-2 (?) BC:  Jesus was born

1 BC:  Herod died (transcripts of Josephus' Antiquities dating before 1544 show that all modern transcripts have had a transcriptional error that erroneously dated Herod's death at 4 BC)

30-33 AD:  Jesus' ministry and death on the cross

66-70 AD:  The Jewish War: Jerusalem sacked and temple destroyed by Roman legions under Vespasian and then his son Titus

132-136 AD: final Jewish insurrection led by Bar Kochba and Jews expelled from Judea by the Romans

130-330 AD: "Late" Roman rule of Palestine, Jews remained in Galilee

330-638 AD: Byzantine Rule (Division of Roman Empire into Eastern and Western Empires)

639-1099 AD: Arab Caliphate Rule

1099-1244 AD: Crusaders Rule; Jews in Jerusalem massacred by Christian Crusaders

1244-1517 AD: Mamluk Rule

1517-1917 AD: 400 years of Ottoman Empire Rule; Jews were still in Jerusalem. The Holy Land was a backwater of the Empire, and considered a part of Syria

1897 AD: First Zionist Congress, organized by Theodore Herzl, met in Switzerland; The Zionist movement to regain a Jewish homeland in the Holy Land became world-wide hope for Jews

1916: WWI was going badly for England and they promised monetary reward for anyone who helped them by formulating stronger and smokeless gunpowder.

1916: Jewish chemist named Chaim Weizmann provided the formula but rejected money and asked for an international homeland for Jews in the Holy Land

1917: Ottoman Empire defeated in WWI, and England given administrative governance over the Holy Land, which they then began to officially call "Palestine"

1917: Balfour Declaration : England supported a Palestinian homeland for the Jews

<u>1917</u>: about 25,000 Jews lived in Palestine. Initially, the Jews purchased 350,000 acres of land.

<u>1920</u>: San Remo Mandate: Representatives of the triumphant nations after WWI established a mandate dividing "Palestine" into a Jewish state west of the Jordan River and an Arab state east of the river. The Balfour Declaration was included in the mandate.

<u>1922</u>: England included Balfour Declaration in its League of Nations mandate over Palestine; about 83,000 Jews lived in Palestine

<u>1932</u>: about 180,000 Jews lived in Palestine

<u>1935</u>: about 300,000 Jews lived in Palestine

<u>1945</u>: about 500,000 Jews lived in Palestine

<u>1948</u>: On May 14, the British Mandate from WWI ended, and Israel declared itself a new nation. The U.S. and Russia quickly recognized the new nation.

Then the holocaust story came out of Europe after WWII. England no longer supported the new Jewish homeland after the war. The U.N. had been formed and took up the matter of a homeland for the Jews. Note that there were thousands of Jewish refugees in the world at that time. They did not want to go back to Eastern Europe. England issued a decree that favored Arab control over all of Palestine. In defiance of the English resolution, Israel declared itself a nation on May 14, 1948, with David Ben Gurion as Prime Minister, and Chaim Weizmann as President. The U.S. and Russia recognized the new nation, and Israel was admitted into the UN by a vote of 37 to 12. The Russians did not want the exiled Jews to come back into their country.

Today, Israel controls over 8000 square miles of land, and the population is in excess of 5 million. Jews from all over the world continue to pour into Israel.

Read Ezekiel 37 again. This is the most auspicious sign of God today. Without God's Hand, Israel would never have become a nation today. This confirms not only the reality of God, but the truth in His prophecies.

# Fig Leaf #16:

# The Land of Israel will Blossom

The Second Sign of Ezekiel is the "Blossoming" of the land of Israel. While this will ultimately be fulfilled in the Millennial Kingdom, it is occurring even today. All around the world, especially around the Sahara desert, we are seeing green lands turning into desert. But only in Israel are we seeing desert being turned into green lands with lush vegetation. The Israelis are using drip irrigation and other techniques to greatly increase the bounty of vegetation in that land. But God has not forgotten Israel. The following biblical passages describe how Israel will ultimately look.

"*For the Lord your God is bringing you into a good land, a land of brooks of water, of fountains and springs, flowing forth in valleys and hills; a land of wheat and barley, of vines and fig trees and pomegranates, a land of olive oil and honey; a land where you will eat food without scarcity, in which you will not lack anything; a land whose stones are iron, and out of whose hills you can dig copper. When you have eaten and are satisfied, you shall bless the Lord your God for the good land which He has given you.*" Deuteronomy 8:7-10

The above verses by Moses describe the land as promised to the Israelites. The prophet Isaiah also foresaw the goodness of the land as promised by God. After foreseeing the destruction of not only Judah, but its neighbors, Isaiah gave the nation a vision of a wonderful future:

"*They shall possess it forever; from generation to generation they will dwell in it. The wilderness and the desert will be glad, and the Arabah will rejoice and blossom; like the crocus it will blossom profusely and rejoice with rejoicing and shout of joy....*

*For waters will break forth in the wilderness and streams*

*in the Arabah. The scorched land will become a pool and the thirsty ground springs of water; in the haunt of jackals, its resting place, grass becomes reeds and rushes."* <u>Isaiah 34:17b; 35:1,6-7</u>[45]

In the chapters letting the nation of Judah know that God still loved and cared for them, and would restore their land, Isaiah encouraged them with the following prophecies:

*"The poor and needy search for water, but there is none; their tongues are parched with thirst. But I the LORD will answer them;*

*I, the God of Israel, will not forsake them. I will make rivers flow on barren heights, and springs within the valleys. I will turn the desert into pools of water, and the parched ground into springs. I will put in the desert the cedar and the acacia, the myrtle and the olive. I will set junipers in the wasteland, the fir and the cypress together,*

*so that people may see and know, may consider and understand, that the hand of the LORD has done this, that the Holy One of Israel has created it."* <u>Isaiah 41:17-20</u>

The following verse looks forward to a lush and bountiful Israel.

*"...I will make a roadway in the wilderness and rivers in the desert.*

*The beasts of the field will glorify Me, the jackals and the ostriches, because I have given waters in the wilderness and rivers in the desert, to give drink to My chosen people."* <u>Isaiah 43:19-20</u>

---

[45] <u>The Bible</u>, God by many authors: *"The wilderness and the desert will be glad, and the Arabah will rejoice and blossom; like the crocus it will blossom profusely and rejoice with rejoicing and shout of joy. The glory of Lebanon will be given to it, the majesty of Carmel and Sharon. They will see the glory of the Lord, the majesty of our God. Encourage the exhausted, and strengthen the feeble. Say to those with anxious heart, 'Take courage, fear not. Behold, your God will come with vengeance; the recompense of God will come, but He will save you.' Then the eyes of the blind will be opened and the ears of the deaf will be unstopped. Then the lame will leap like a deer, and the tongue of the mute will shout for joy. For waters will break forth in the wilderness and streams in the Arabah. The scorched land will become a pool and the thirsty ground springs of water; in the haunt of jackals, its resting place, grass becomes reeds and rushes."* <u>Isaiah 35:1-7</u>

This verse could have layered meanings with literal water, and of course the coming of Yeshua, the Messiah to give spiritual drink to God's people.

Ezekiel also was shown the lushness of God's grace on the land of Israel:

*"I will feed them in a good pasture, and their grazing ground will be on the mountain heights of Israel. There they will lie down on good grazing ground and feed in rich pasture on the mountains of Israel.*

*I will make them and the places around My hill a blessing. And I will cause showers to come down in their season; they will be showers of blessing.*

*Also the tree of the field will yield its fruit and the earth will yield its increase, and they will be secure on their land. Then they will know that I am the Lord, when I have broken the bars of their yoke and have delivered them from the hand of those who enslaved them.*

*I will establish for them a renowned planting place, and they will not again be victims of famine in the land, and they will not endure the insults of the nations anymore."* <u>Ezekiel 34:14,26-27,29</u>

This prophecy seems to be partially fulfilled at this time. There has been some scholarly evidence of marked increase in rainfall in Israel since the 1920s. However, the area still suffers from drought at times. The fullness of the rain and return of the land to an almost Eden-like garden state will most likely occur during the Millennium, and afterward when the earth is re-created.

*"Moreover, I will save you from all your uncleanness; and I will call for the grain and multiply it, and I will not bring a famine on you.*

*I will multiply the fruit of the tree and the produce of the field, so that you will not receive again the disgrace of famine among the nations.*

*The desolate land will be cultivated instead of being a desolation in the sight of everyone who passes by.*

*They will say, 'This desolate land has become like the garden of Eden; and the waste, desolate and ruined cities are fortified and inhabited.'*

*Then the nations that are left round about you will know that I, the Lord, have rebuilt the ruined places and planted that which was desolate; I, the Lord, have spoken and will do it."* Ezekiel 36:29-30, 34-36

These verses describe the flourishing and bounteousness that God will bring to the restored land of Israel.

Zechariah again reaffirms the land as the inheritance that God has given them.

*"The seed will grow well, the vine will yield its fruit, the ground will produce its crops, and the heavens will drop their dew. I will give all these things as an inheritance to the remnant of this people."* Zechariah 8:12

*"The days are coming," declares the LORD, "when the reaper will be overtaken by the plowman and the planter by the one treading grapes. New wine will drip from the mountains and flow from all the hills"* Amos 9:13

Both of the previous verses look toward a bounteous restored Israel.

**An important concept here is that God promises to bless the land of Israel AND the Jewish people when they are both together!** One only has to read the dreadful condition of the land in the 1860s as described by Mark Twain in *Innocents Abroad* and then see the flourishing land of Israel today to get the full impact of this concept. Twain described a desolate land with areas of malaria-ridden marshes and a few squalid villages of Arabs in that time before the Jews began to return to the land.[46] Today, through the efforts of the

---

[46] Innocents Abroad, Mark Twain. 1869: "Of all the lands there are for dismal scenery, I think Palestine must be the prince. The hills are barren,

forestation and reforestation programs of the Israelis, the land is green and bounteous—right up to the borders of its neighboring countries. This is truly one of the great miracles of our time, and another of the great signs, or Fig Leaves, occurring right in front of us. The final verses of Amos which follow the one above show God's heart for His people and THEIR land.

>  "'*Also I will restore the captivity of My people Israel (NASB)[I will bring back my exiled people Israel (NIV)] and they will rebuild the ruined cities and live in them; they will also plant vineyards and drink their wine, and make gardens and eat their fruit. I will also plant them on **their** land which I have given them,' says the Lord your God.*" Amos 9:14-15

The emphasis here is that this is the land given to the Jews by God. The current position that this has been the home of Palestinians for hundreds of years is not really supported by the facts. All during the reign of the Malmuks and Ottomans, the land was neglected and inhabited by small bands of Arabs who called themselves "Syrians". A few Jews, Arabs and Christians lived in the cities of Jerusalem[47] and Tiberias, but most of the land was desolate. Only when the Ottoman Empire was destroyed in World War I, and the English became the administrators of the region did Arabs and

---

they are dull of color, they are unpicturesque in shape. The valleys are unsightly deserts fringed with a feeble vegetation that has an expression about it of being sorrowful and despondent. The Dead Sea and the Sea of Galilee sleep in the midst of a vast stretch of hill and plain wherein the eye rests upon no pleasant tint, no striking object, no soft picture dreaming in a purple haze or mottled with the shadows of the clouds. Every outline is harsh, every feature is distinct, there is no perspective—distance works no enchantment here. It is a hopeless, dreary, heart-broken land." (Chap. 56).

[47] Innocents Abroad, Mark Twain, 1869. "The population of Jerusalem is composed of Muslims, Jews, Greeks, Latins, Armenians, Syrians, Copts, Abyssinians, Greek Catholics, and a handful of Protestants. One hundred of the latter sect are all that dwell now in this birthplace of Christianity. The nice shades of nationality comprised in the above list, and the languages spoken by them, are altogether too numerous to mention. It seems to me that all the races and colors and tongues of the earth must be represented among the fourteen thousand souls that dwell in Jerusalem." (Chap. 56).

Jews begin to re-populate the area. So the claim of "long-standing" ownership by so-called Palestinians is political fodder only, and not based on truth. In fact, the British Embassy noted in 1860 that Jews were the majority population in Jerusalem at that time.

# Fig Leaf #17:

# Israel Will Prosper

The Third Sign in Ezekiel is that Israel will prosper. God will bless the restored land of Israel with great prosperity. This is already partially fulfilled as the land yields more vegetables and fruits for export.  Also, the economy of Israel has become one of the strongest in the Mideast.

Businesses are thriving, and the education level of the population is the highest in the area.  Many Israelis are now millionaires, and there is very little poverty in the country. The Israelis are blessed by God, and have an innate, God-given ability to create new things.  One of the strongest elements of the Israeli economy is the segment of intellectual property.  In contrast, Lebanon, once a very prosperous country, continues to try to regain some economic momentum.  However, the continued occupation by Hezbollah has made rebuilding almost impossible.  Israel's prosperity continues to irritate the surrounding Muslims.  As God arranges the upcoming events, look for the prosperity of Israel to increase.

*"I will make them and the places around My hill a blessing.  And I will cause showers to come down in their season; they will be showers of blessing.  And the tree of the field will yield its fruit and the earth will yield its increase, and they will be secure on their land.  Then they will know that I am the Lord...*
*I will establish for them a renowned planting place, and they will not again be victims of famine in the land, and they will not endure the insults of the nations anymore."* <u>Ezekiel 34:26-27a,29</u>

*"But you, O mountains of Israel, you will put forth your branches and bear your fruit for My people Israel; for they will soon come.  For, behold, I am for you, and I will turn to you, and*

*you will be cultivated and sown. I will multiply men on you, all the house of Israel, all of it; and the cities will be inhabited and the waste places will be rebuilt. I will multiply on you man and beast; and they will increase and be fruitful; and I will cause you to be inhabited as you were formerly and will treat you better than at the first, Thus you will know that I am the Lord."* <u>Ezekiel 36: 8-11</u>

In today's economies around the world, oil and gas are extremely important as energy sources. The Israelis are leading the world with innovative use of sun, wind, and water as sources of energy. But these technologies are still in their infancy and the Israeli economy requires the oil and gas like other economies.

Golda Meir was Prime Minister of Israel from 1969 to 1974. She was famous for her lament, "Let me tell you something that we Israelis have against Moses. He took us 40 years through the desert in order to bring us to the one spot in the Middle East that has no oil!"

But maybe Moses knew something that Golda did not. Listen to Moses' blessings on the tribes of Israel.

<u>Deuteronomy 33:13:</u> *Of Joseph he said, "Blessed of the Lord be his land, with the choice things of heaven, with the dew,* **and from the deep lying beneath**.*"*

<u>Deuteronomy 33:18-19:</u> *Of Zebulun he said, "Rejoice, Zebulun, in your going forth, and, Issachar, in your tents. They will call peoples to the mountain; there they will offer righteous sacrifices; for they will draw out the abundance of the seas, and* **the hidden treasures of the sand**.*"*

Moses was pronouncing blessings on the tribes of Israel. Each tribe was to have its own territory, and Moses seemed to imply that there were some "treasures" hidden in the lands of the tribes of Joseph, Zebulun and Issachar. Many have interpreted these verses to indicate that there is oil below Israel. Several oil companies are now engaged in looking for oil beneath the country of Israel.

Zion Oil, a Christian-based company has drilling rights from Carmel to the Sea of Galilee, and has begun to sink test wells in that area, based on Scriptures. The lands allotted to Zebulun and Manassas, son of Joseph, encompass the area around the Jezreel valley where Zion Oil is searching for possible oil deposits.

In 1995, a small oil field containing an estimated 11-12 million barrels of crude oil was found west of the Dead Sea, but was not drilled due to cost prohibitions. This area has been leased to several oil drilling companies, and is expected to begin production soon.

In 2015, a much larger field was found in the southern Golan Heights area that is expected to yield large amounts of oil in the near future.

Historically, Israel relied on external imports for meeting most of its energy needs, spending an amount equivalent to over 5% of its GDP per year in 2009 on imports of energy products. In the late 1990s, the government of Israel decided to encourage the usage of natural gas because of environmental and regional resources. Although there were no oil or gas fields in Israel at that time, a pipeline was being built from Egypt that would supply natural gas. This pipeline supply was disrupted by jihadists in 2012, which caused economic harm to Israel at that time.

A small gas field was found off-shore of Ashkelon in 2000 that helped supply Israel, but was almost totally depleted by 2014 due to the interruption of the Egyptian pipeline. In 2009, a huge gas field, which the government named "Tamar", was found in deep water about 60 miles west of Haifa and a smaller field just off-shore. Another gigantic gas field just beyond the huge Tamar gas field has been located and is twice

as large as the current field.  It has been named "Leviathan."
The Leviathan gas field operations have begun pumping
natural gas to Israel as of 2017, and will be fully operational by
2019.  Subsequently, Israel has plenty of natural gas, and is
actually exporting gas.

Another gas field has been found off the southern
coast, and has been named the "Daniel" field.  It appears to be
the same size as the Tamar field, and will continue to provide
more natural gas for the country.

God has indeed blessed Israel, and the country will
continue to prosper.

# Fig Leaf #18:

# Israel Will Be Secure

The next sign in Ezekiel is that Israel will be secure. Many who study prophecy state that this will come during the Millennium.  Others state that this will occur during the first part of the Tribulation when the Anti-Christ makes a covenant with Israel ensuring the country's peace.  However, the implications of the scripture tend to indicate that Israel is at peace when the Russo-Iranian invasion occurs (See Fig Leaf #19).  This could happen as the Israeli-Palestinian peace accords go forth.

The Oslo Accords agreement was signed by Israel and the Palestinian Authority in 1993, and was to lead to further negotiations toward Palestinian autonomy.  However, the various Palestinian organizations such as the PLO and Hamas have repeatedly failed to uphold their end of the pact, and have continued to attack Israelis during their infatadas.  Even without the façade of an infatada, these organizations openly urge their constituents to kill and maim Jews when they can.  The Israeli government leaders since then have given multiple concessions to the Palestinians, such as governance and authority over Gaza and the West Bank.  But the Palestinian authorities have used all of these efforts to increase their negative rhetoric toward Israel, and still declare that Israel must be dissolved as a nation.

Incredibly, the Palestinians, who were given back the Temple Mount after the 1967 Six-Day War, have now taken the position that there never was a Jewish temple on that site. Jerusalem and the Mount were captured by the Jordanian army in 1948, during the Arab war against the new Jewish state.  The city and the Mount were then captured by the

118

Israelis in the 1967 war by General Moshe Dayan. As a peace gesture, the Israelis returned the Mount back to the Muslims since the Al-Aksa mosque still stands there, as well as the Dome of the Rock. Today it is under Palestinian jurisdiction. The modern Muslim leaders now stridently declare that there was never a Jewish Temple on that site! Today, if someone ascends to the top of the Mount, one cannot have any literature that has any reference to a Jewish Temple there, nor can anyone pray or express any religious expression that is not Muslim. Any such expressions will result in the "offender" being expelled from the Mount by guards.

The "Road to Peace in the Mideast" begun by President George W. Bush, and continued by his successor(s) includes the demand for the establishment of a Palestinian country inside of the current state of Israel. Many Israelis and their leaders have agreed to this concept. It has always been the Palestinians and their Arab backers who reject the "Two State" solution because they reject Israel's right to remain a country. The problem of how to ensure that a new country within the boundaries of Israel will not become a staging area for further attacks on Israel by Palestinians remains the utmost concern for the Israeli leaders. Survey after survey has shown that while the Israelis have no problem living side by side with the Palestinians in peace, many Palestinian citizens repeatedly voice the sentiment that they want to kill every Israeli in the area. (While visiting in Israel, I did meet Palestinians who long for peace, and do not voice the sentiment of wanting to kill Israelis.) As long as the total destruction of the nation of Israel remains the sentiment of the most vocal Palestinians, the "Road to Peace in the Mideast" remains in jeopardy.

However tentative peace appears to outsiders, in reality most Israelis live their day to day lives with great security. They do not seem to go about in fear at all. The Israeli military is the dominant force in the area. Many Americans who have seen the Israeli military armaments are amazed at the improvements that the Israelis have made to the equipment that America has sold them. The Israelis also excel in producing their own excellent equipment. It is a God-given "gift" that the Jews have.

The Israeli Defense Force fierceness brings to mind the words of Zechariah 12:6

*"In that day I will make the clans of Judah like a firepot among pieces of wood and a flaming torch among sheaves, so they will consume on the right hand and on the left all the surrounding peoples, while the inhabitants of Jerusalem again dwell on their own sites in Jerusalem."*

Read these promises from God's Word regarding the peace and security of Israel:

*"This is what the Sovereign LORD says: 'When I gather the people of Israel from the nations where they have been scattered, I will be proved holy through them in the sight of the nations. Then they will live in their own land, which I gave to my servant Jacob. They will live there in safety and will build houses and plant vineyards; **they will live in safety** when I inflict punishment on all their neighbors who maligned them. Then they will know that I am the LORD their God.'"* Ezekiel 28:25, 26

*"I myself will tend my sheep and have them lie down, declares the Sovereign LORD.... I will make a covenant of peace with them and rid the land of savage beasts so that they may live in the wilderness and sleep in the forests in safety...**They will no longer be plundered by the nations**, nor will wild animals devour them. **They will live in safety, and no one will make them afraid.**"* Ezekiel 34:15, 25, 28

Ezekiel described how the inhabitants of Israel would be secure when the invasion of Magog occurs, as described below.

*"...whose people were gathered from many nations to the mountains of Israel, which had long been desolate. They had been brought out from the nations, and now all of them **live in safety.***

*...You will say, "I will invade a land of unwalled villages; I will attack a peaceful and unsuspecting people—all of them living without walls and without gates and bars*
*....Therefore, son of man, prophesy and say to Gog: 'This is what the Sovereign LORD says: In that day, when my people Israel are living in safety, will you not take notice of it?"* Ezekiel 38: 8, 11, 14

The prophet Isaiah foresaw and knew from where Israel's peace and security will come. *"Lord, you will establish peace for us..."* Isaiah 26: 12

While Hamas and Hezbollah continue to try to wipe Israel from the face of the earth, God continues to shield and guard His chosen people. As He said, not for their sake, but for His: *"It is not for your sake, O house of Israel, that I am about to act, but for My holy name"* Ezekiel 36:22

From 2001 to 2014, over 20,000 missiles and rockets were fired at Israel from the Gaza Strip. An article written during Operation Protective Edge in 2014 noted that during that short period of time 3,356 rockets had been fired from Gaza into Israel. 578 rockets had been intercepted by Israel's Iron Dome defense system—roughly 17 % of those fired. Iron Dome operators told about miracles occurring involving the missiles being "pushed" off course while in the air. As one of the terrorists from Gaza was reported to say when asked why they couldn't aim their rockets more effectively: 'We do aim them, but their God changes their path in mid-air.'

Israel Today, a news agency in Israel, translated a report from a Hebrew-language news site. The article carried an Israeli commander's report about an incoming rocket headed toward Tel Aviv during the Protective Edge offensive (2014). The commander recalled: 'A missile was fired from Gaza. Iron Dome precisely calculated [its trajectory]. 'We know where these missiles are going to land down to a radius of 200 meters. This particular missile was going to hit either the Azrieli Towers, the Kirya (Israel's equivalent of the Pentagon) or [a central Tel Aviv railway station]. Hundreds could have died. 'We fired the first [interceptor]. It missed. Second [interceptor]. It missed. This is very rare. I was in shock. 'Suddenly, Iron Dome (which calculates wind speeds, among other things) shows a major wind coming from the east, a strong wind that ... sends the missile into the sea. We were all stunned. I stood up and shouted, 'There is a God!,' he said. 'I witnessed this miracle with my own eyes. It was not told or reported to me. I saw the hand of God send that missile into the sea.'[48]

God will continue to prosper and protect His people and their land. The establishment of Israel in 1948 was a God-ordained miracle. The continued protection of His people is part of His plan. There will be a time when the entire nation of Israel will be put into a great trial—the time known in the Scriptures as "Jacob's Trouble." We call that time "The Tribulation." The Israeli people will be tested to the extreme, but God will salvage a remnant who will then be the Premier people living in the Premier kingdom in the world

One of the greatest displays of God's protection of Israel will come when Iran and Russia put together a huge army to destroy the country.

48  www.dailymail.co.uk/.../Hand_God_prevents-rocket-striking-target-Israeli-Iron-Dome, 6 August 2014

# Fig Leaf #19:

# The "Magog" Invasion

The fifth sign revealed in Ezekiel is the great invasion by Magog. Chapters 38 and 39 describe this event very clearly. First, the Bible calls by name the nations who will invade Israel.

*"The word of the LORD came to me: "Son of man, set your face against Gog, of the land of Magog, the chief prince of Meshek and Tubal; prophesy against him and say:*
*'This is what the Sovereign LORD says: I am against you, Gog, chief prince of Meshek and Tubal. I will turn you around, put hooks in your jaws and bring you out with your whole army—your horses, your horsemen fully armed, and a great horde with large and small shields, all of them brandishing their swords.*
*Persia, Cush and Put will be with them, all with shields and helmets, also Gomer with all its troops, and Beth Togarmah from the far north with all its troops—the many nations with you."* <u>Ezekiel 38:1-6</u>

Since Gog is called the prince of Rosh, Meschech and Tubal, we know that this name refers to a person who will lead this army. He is said to be from Magog. Extensive investigation over the past centuries of where Magog might be has usually led to the conclusion that Magog is now Russia. In <u>verse 2 of chapter 39</u>, the prophet, Ezekiel, notes that Gog will come from the remotest parts of the north:
*"Behold, I am against you, O Gog, prince of Rosh, Meshech and Tubal; and I will turn you around, drive you on, take you up from the remotest parts of the north and bring you against the mountains of Israel."*

If one goes straight north from Israel, he will pass through Lebanon, Syria, Turkey, and then over the Black Sea

123

into Russia. Rosh has been best interpreted to mean Russia, and Meshech has arguably been deemed as referring to Moscow. The best explanation has to do with the descendants of Noah's son, Japheth. Genesis 10:2 lists his sons as Gomer, Magog, Madai, Javan, Tubal, Meshech, and Tiras. One of Gomer's son was Togarmah. Traditionally, Magog and the others went North after the dispersion of the peoples over the earth. The Scythians were considered their descendants and populated the areas around the Black Sea. The Russians are the descendants of Magog, while Gomer, Tubal, Meschech refer to other descendants from the Black Sea areas. Look at the newly formed countries around the southern part of Russia. These countries are almost all Muslim, and the peoples are the descendants of the Scythians. No doubt armies from these countries will be involved in the Magog invasion.

Persia was the name of the country east of Iraq until 1935, when it changed its name to Iran. Russia is building an alliance with Iran. It is selling Iran military materiel and the materials needed to be a nuclear power. Put is described as the founder of Libya. Ethiopia (Cush) refers to the area called Sudan now, as well as the area we call Ethiopia. Since the areas described are mostly Muslim now, and Russia has a large Muslim population, we can see how this army might be deployed against Israel. Joel Rosenberg also notes that this alliance is significant in which countries are not listed.[49] He notes that 20-30 years ago, everyone would have thought that Egypt and Iraq would be the most likely countries to attack Israel. But today, these two countries are at relative peace with Israel while Iran and its allies—including Hezbollah—continue to bluster about wiping Israel off of the face of the earth.

Gog will bring a great army of many peoples against Israel:

*"After many days you will be called to arms. In future*

---

[49] Epicenter, Joel Rosenberg, Tyndale House Publishers, Inc., 2006, p.132

*years you will invade a land that has recovered from war, whose people were gathered from many nations to the mountains of Israel, which had long been desolate.*

*They had been brought out from the nations, and now all of them live in safety. You and all your troops and the many nations with you will go up, advancing like a storm; you will be like a cloud covering the land."* <u>Ezekiel 38:8-9</u>

The people living in Israel will have been gathered from all over the world and living in safety (Ezek. 38:8). Gog's army will array itself against Israel and will be massive (Ezekiel 38:9). Gog will devise his plan to attack those who are living in security and "capture spoil and to seize plunder:"

*"You will say, "I will invade a land of unwalled villages; I will attack a peaceful and unsuspecting people—all of them living without walls and without gates and bars.*

*I will plunder and loot and turn my hand against the resettled ruins and the people gathered from the nations, rich in livestock and goods, living at the center of the land."* <u>Ezekiel 38:11-12</u>

The next verse has several interpretations.

*"Sheba and Dedan and the merchants of Tarshish with all its villages will say to you, "Have you come to capture spoil? Have you assembled your company to seize plunder, to carry away silver and gold, to take away cattle and goods, to capture great spoil?""* <u>Ezekiel 38:13</u>

Some have said that these are the neighbors of Israel who trade with them and are interested in the great army's motive. Some think that these traders then join in the great invasion. Others think that this may illustrate Israel's friends, such as the U.S., who try to negotiate with Russia and Iran. But when Gog and his army are ready to invade Israel, none of Israel's "friends" will help defend it. God Himself will rise up and defend the land:

*"'This is what the Sovereign LORD says: You are the one I spoke of in former days by my servants the prophets of Israel. At*

*that time they prophesied for years that I would bring you against them. This is what will happen in that day: When Gog attacks the land of Israel, my hot anger will be aroused, declares the Sovereign LORD."* Ezekiel 38:17-18

First there will be a massive earthquake that will shake the entire earth and throw down the mountains of Israel.

*"In My zeal and in My blazing wrath I declare that on that day there will surely be a great earthquake in the land of Israel. The fish of the sea, the birds of the heavens, the beasts of the field, all the creeping things that creep on the earth, and all the men who are on the face of the earth will shake at My presence; the mountains also will be thrown down, the steep pathways will collapse and every wall will fall to the ground."* Ezekiel 38:19-20

Next, the factions of the army will turn upon each other.
*"I will call for a sword against him on all My mountains,"* declares the Lord God, *"every man's sword will be against his brother."* Ezekiel 38:21

Then God will bring a torrential rain on the great army, filled with hailstones, fire and brimstone.
*"With pestilence and with blood I will enter into judgment with him; and I will rain on him and on his troops, and on the many peoples who are with him, a torrential rain, with hailstones, fire and brimstone."* Ezekiel 38:22

The great army will be destroyed. All weapons and aircraft will be knocked to the ground, miraculously falling on the mountains and in the open fields.

*"Then I will strike your bow from your left hand and make your arrows drop from your right hand. On the mountains of Israel you will fall, you and all your troops and the nations with you. I will give you as food to all kinds of carrion birds and to the wild animals. You will fall in the open field, for I have spoken, declares the Sovereign LORD."* Ezekiel 39:3-5

This great sign will demonstrate God's power to the world.  In my opinion, it will also confuse the Muslims.  All of their lives they have been taught that their god (Allah) wants them to destroy Israel.  Right in front of their eyes, they will witness God's protection of Israel, and the destruction of the great Muslim army.  They will undoubtedly be very spiritually confused.  The Israelis will use the destroyed weapons for energy production for the next seven years.

*"Then those who inhabit the cities of Israel will go out and make fires with the weapons and burn them, both shields and bucklers, bows and arrows, war clubs and spears, and for seven years they will make fires of them."* <u>Ezekiel 39:9</u>

The remains of the army will be buried east of the Sea of Galilee, or perhaps east of the Dead Sea.  The earthquake could open up new valleys.

*"On that day I will give Gog a burial ground there in Israel, the valley of those who pass by east of the sea, and it will block off those who would pass by.  So they will bury Gog there with all his horde, and they will call it the valley of Hamon-gog."* <u>Ezekiel 39:11</u>

It will take the Israelis seven months to bury the dead. *"For seven months the house of Israel will be burying them in order to cleanse the land."* <u>Ezekiel 39:12</u>

Russia, the rising superpower, and its partner, Iran, will at that time have no effective military forces.  This will leave a power vacuum in the Middle East, setting the stage for the new World Government.  The confused Muslims in the area will be ripe for following after the Anti-Christ and his False Prophet.

# Isaiah:

# Egypt & Assyria

These next two events will happen during the Second Coming of Jesus and afterwards, but I am including them in this discussion as a interesting commentary on how God feels about other countries than Israel. Of note, the two countries discussed, Egypt and Assyria (Syria and Iraq in today's world), are not listed as being part of the Magog/Gog invasion.

# Fig Leaf #20:

# Egypt Will Be Saved By Jesus

Chapter 19 of Isaiah ties in to this discussion due to the countries mentioned.  The first prophesy will be "late", occurring in the "Day of the Lord" (during the tribulation), and the other will be fulfilled during the Millennium.  In verses 1-4, the time frame of this chapter is placed just before the Second Coming of the Lord late in the Tribulation:

*"Behold, the Lord is riding on a swift cloud and is about to come to Egypt; the idols of Egypt will tremble at His presence, and the heart of the Egyptians will melt within them."* Isaiah 19:1

Egyptians will fight against each other and begin to resort to idols, ghosts, mediums and people who call upon the "spirits" to help them:

*"So I will incite Egyptians against Egyptians; and they will each fight against his brother and each against his neighbor, city against city and kingdom against kingdom.  Then the spirit of the Egyptians will be demoralized within them; and I will confound their strategy, so they will resort to idols and ghosts of the dead and to mediums and spiritists."*  Isaiah19:2-3

God will deliver them into the *"...hand of a cruel master, and a mighty king will rule over them"* (v. 4).  The timing and the spiritual chaos pictured in these verses suggest a time after the failed invasion of Gog and Magog.  The stunned Muslims could be confused and might revert to paganist worship patterns.  Then a cruel King will rise up and take over Egypt.

*"Moreover, I will deliver the Egyptians into the hand of a cruel master, and a mighty king will rule over them,"* declares the Lord God of hosts. Isaiah 19:4

The cruel master is probably the King of the South, and the mighty king would be the Anti-Christ. In Daniel 11:40-43, a battle between the King of the South and the Anti-Christ is described. The King of the South (Egypt?) will attack the Anti-Christ, who then will destroy the King of the South and enter into Egypt and take over with the Libyans (Put) and Sudanese (Cush) at his side.[50]

Isaiah then describes a terrible drought that dries up the river of Egypt[51] and which will destroy the country economically:

*And the fishermen will lament, and all those who cast a line into the Nile will mourn, and those who spread nets on the waters will pine away. Moreover, the manufacturers of linen made from combed flax and the weavers of white cloth will be utterly dejected. And the pillars of Egypt will be crushed; all the hired laborers will be grieved in soul. There will be no work for Egypt which its head or tail, its palm branch or bulrush, may do.* Isaiah 19:8-10,15

This great drought will probably occur during the Great Tribulation, when the Great Bowl Judgments will be poured out on the earth. We are told that the sun will greatly increase its heat, and that the Euphrates River will dry up. At that time, the Nile will undoubtedly dry up also.

---

[50] The Bible, God through many authors; *"At the end time the king of the South will collide with him, and the king of the North will storm against him with chariots, with horsemen and with many ships; and he will enter countries, overflow them and pass through. He will also enter the Beautiful Land, and many countries will fall; but these will be rescued out of his hand: Edom, Moab and the foremost of the sons of Ammon. Then he will stretch out his hand against other countries, and the land of Egypt will not escape. But he will gain control over the hidden treasures of gold and silver and over all the precious things of Egypt; and Libyans and Ethiopians will follow at his heels."* Daniel 11:40-43

[51] The Bible, God through many authors; *The waters from the sea will dry up, and the river will be parched and dry. The canals will emit a stench, the streams of Egypt will thin out and dry up; the reeds and rushes will rot away. The bulrushes by the Nile, by the edge of the Nile and all the sown fields by the Nile will become dry, be driven away, and be no more.* Isaiah 19:5-7

The Egyptians will then be in great fear of the Lord:

*In that day the Egyptians will become like women, and they will tremble and be in dread because of the waving of the hand of the Lord of hosts, which he is going to wave over them.* Isaiah 19:16

They will also fear Israel:
*The land of Judah will become a terror to Egypt; everyone to whom it is mentioned will be in dread of it, because of the purpose of the Lord of hosts which He is purposing against them.* Isaiah19:17

Five Egyptian cities will turn to the Lord and begin to speak Hebrew:
*In that day five cities in the land of Egypt will be speaking the language of Canaan and swearing allegiance to the Lord of hosts; one will be called the City of Destruction/Sun.* Isaiah 19:18

In the middle of the country will rise a church to worship the Lord, undoubtedly through special revelation to the Egyptians,

*"In that day there will be an altar to the Lord in the midst of the land of Egypt, and a pillar to the Lord near its border."* Isaiah 19:19

Then God will send a Savior (Jesus) into the country and save them from their oppressors:
*"It will become a sign and witness to the Lord of hosts in the land of Egypt; for they will cry to the Lord because of oppressors, and he will send them a Savior and a Champion, and He will deliver them. Thus the Lord will make Himself known to Egypt, and the Egyptians will know the Lord in that day. They will even worship with sacrifice and offering, and will make a vow to the Lord and perform it."* Isaiah 19:20-21

This refers to Jesus entering the country and destroying the forces of the Anti-Christ. Given the events noted in other prophecy, Jesus will probably intervene in Egypt during His Second Coming, ending the Day of the Lord. In verse 22, the Lord will strike Egypt during His destruction of the Anti-Christ's armies, but will then heal the country *"The Lord will strike Egypt, striking but healing; so they will return to the Lord, and He will respond to them and will heal them."* Isaiah 19:22

# Fig Leaf #21:

# A Highway From Egypt to Assyria

The next great sign noted in this chapter (Isaiah 19) is a highway running from Egypt to Iraq (Assyria). We're told in verse 23 that the Iraqis and Egyptians will travel this highway between their two countries in order to worship God together.

*"In that day there will be a highway from Egypt to Assyria, and the Assyrians will come into Egypt and the Egyptians into Assyria, and the Egyptians will worship with the Assyrians."* Isaiah19:23

Then we are told that Israel will be included with Egypt and Iraq as a blessing in the center of the world.

*"In that day Israel will be the third party with Egypt and Assyria, a blessing in the midst of the earth."* Isaiah 19:24

And the Lord declares, *"Blessed is Egypt My people, and Assyria the work of My hands, and Israel My inheritance"* Isaiah 19:25

The most probable timing for this would be during the Millennium, since Jesus does enter the country before the highway is mentioned. It is amazing that the two countries which do not join in the Russian-Iranian attack on Israel become God's blessings in the world, and are named by Him as blessed along with Israel.

These then are the twenty-one prophecies that point to the future of the world as revealed by God through his prophets and through His Son, Jesus (Yeshua). There are many more prophecies regarding the future that are parts of the Christian Eschatology.

# SECTION II

## END TIME EVENTS

### Christian Eschatology

# CHAPTER 6

# Prologue

The essential teachings of Christian eschatology have been given previously in Section 1 of this book. The next events to happen before the Tribulation are the Rapture of the Church, and the Magog Invasion of Israel. After the Church is taken off the earth, and the Muslim religion has been thrown into disarray by the divine defeat of that great army of Magog, the world will ride into the Tribulation on the five great waves of history: Culture, Religion, Economics, Politics, and Technology.

Culturally, without any Christian influence, the world will continue to march away from God's ordinances, congratulating itself on its tolerance and inclusiveness while further embracing more and more degradations as "normal." Religiously, the movement for more inclusiveness will move people toward a more "tolerant" world religion that will relegate all human actions, ideologies, thoughts, and emotions as acceptable. All religions will be syncretized into a World-wide Religion. Economically, capitalism will be abolished as the powerful operators of the world consolidate the disparate economies into one world-wide socialist economy. As with all historical socialism, freedoms will be taken away from the common citizens, and power accruing to the few at the top.

Politically, a great commonwealth government will rise in an effort to provide a single governance of all peoples. The world's countries will be divided into ten areas, with a "governor" or "commissioner" as leader of each particular area. These ten people will govern the world as the top ruling body. A charming but devious man will begin to build power, and will become one of these governors. He will be able to resolve conflicts and will become more and more powerful in the eyes of the world's citizens. He will be the final and great "Anti-Christ." He will eventually become the tyrant over the world government, and will also require everyone to worship him as "god."

Technologically, travel and communications will continue to develop at blazing speeds. New technology will enable people to travel more rapidly, while cultural degradations will make people fear to travel to more areas of the world. Communications capabilities will continue to follow Moore's Law[52], and increase each year. However, when the world has moved into the Tribulation, and God's judgments are beginning, human efforts will be shunted into growing and producing food, and fighting the wars that the Anti-Christ will wage against his opponents.

At the end of the Tribulation period, Jesus will return to earth in His position as King of Kings, and Lord of Lords. He will defeat the Anti-Christ's large army (Armageddon) and establish His Millennial Kingdom on earth.

---

[52] Wikipedia: Moore's law is the observation that the number of transistors in a dense integrated circuit doubles about every two years...Moore's prediction proved accurate for several decades, and has been used in the semiconductor industry to guide long-term planning and to set targets for research and development.

# CHAPTER 7

# The Rapture

The Rapture is that great event where the Church is caught up in the air with Jesus. Most evangelical Christians, including messianic Jews, look to the Rapture of the church before the great wrath of the Tribulation. Many evangelicals will be surprised to learn that many theologians do not think there will be a Rapture of the Church until the very end of the Tribulation. Wayne Grudem states that ..."The New Testament nowhere clearly says that the church will be taken out of the world before the tribulation...but... these passages (have) been understood by believers throughout history as speaking not of a secret rapture of the church before the tribulation, but of a very visible public rapture of the church to be with Christ just a few moments prior to his coming to earth with them to reign during the millennial kingdom..."[53] Nevertheless, there are four views held by Christians regarding the timing of the Rapture. First, the **Pre-Tribulation** view states that the Church will be taken out of the world <u>before</u> the seven-year Tribulation. The **Mid-Tribulation** view obviously looks for the Rapture to come after the Anti-Christ

---

[53] <u>Systematic Theology</u>, Wayne Grudem, Zondervan Publishing House, 1994, page 1134

breaks his covenant with Israel three and half years into the Tribulation.  The **Pre-Wrath** view looks for the Rapture just before the "Wrath of God" (the Trumpet and Bowl judgments of Revelation) comes on the earth, and postulate that this would probably occur four to five years into the Tribulation.  The **Post-Tribulation** view follows Grudem's teaching that the Church is not raptured until a few moments before Christ's Glorious Appearance in the Second Coming.

The scriptural basis for the Rapture comes from 1 Thessalonians 1:10, 4:13-18, 5:1-9, 1 Corinthians 15:50-53, and Revelation 3:10.  In 1 Thessalonians 1:10, there is the promise that Jesus "*...rescues us from the wrath to come.*"  Similarly, Jesus says to the church in Philadelphia (Revelation 3:10), that "*...I will keep you from the hour of testing, that hour which is about to come upon the whole world, to test those who dwell on the earth.*"  In 1 Thessalonians 4:17, Paul states "*...Then we who are alive and remain will be caught up together with them in the clouds to meet the Lord in the air...*"  Again in 1 Corinthians 15:51-52 that "*...we will all be changed, in a moment, in the twinkling of an eye, at the last trumpet; for the trumpet will sound, and the dead will be raised imperishable, and we will be changed.*"

These scriptures suggest that the living members of the Church will be changed in a twinkling of an eye, and then caught up with the Lord in the air, before the wrath and testing comes upon the world.  (Some believe that Paul's allusion to the last trumpet actually refers to the seventh Trumpet Judgment, when the final trumpet is sounded just before the seven Bowl Judgments.  This view would then say that the "Day of the Lord" begins at that time, and God's wrath is poured out on the earth in the Bowl Judgments.  Thus the church is saved from God's wrath.)

The Post-Tribulationists believe that the verses above do not actually mean that Jesus will save us from the Tribulation, but are being misinterpreted to mean so.

Obviously the other three views believe that the Church will be rescued before the wrath begins, they just disagree when the "wrath of God" actually begins.

If the Pre-Tribulation view is correct, then once the Church is raptured out of the world, we will not have to worry about "Fig Leaves" anymore. However, if one of the other three views is correct, then the Church will have to continue to watch for further signs leading up to the Second Coming of Jesus. My concern is that good Christians who believe in the Pre-Tribulation Rapture would become disheartened and even possibly "fall away" as Jesus warned if they see the Anti-Christ rising and covenanting with Israel, and the Rapture would not have yet occurred. We must remember that our Lord will not forsake us. No matter how much hardship and how many trials we must endure and persevere, He will be with us, and our reward and joy will be great in the end.

The Rapture also ends the Age of Grace. Since the Holy Spirit came to earth in force during the Feast of Pentecost,[54] fifty days after the Resurrection of Jesus, God's salvation has been available to mankind through the simple act of believing and repenting of one's previous sins. This "easy" salvation, bought for us by the horrendous death of Yeshua (Jesus), comes by way of God's amazing Grace, now available through His Son. This Age of Grace, also called the Church Age, will end when the Church is raptured off this earth.

There also will be an order to the Rapture. Those who have already died in Christ will be caught up in the air with Yeshua first. Rabbi Saul (the Apostle Paul) wrote to the Thessalonians that      *"...For if we believe that Jesus died and*

---

[54] The Bible, God through many authors, *When the day of Pentecost had come, they were all together in one place. And suddenly there came from heaven a noise like a violent rushing wind, and it filled the whole house where they were sitting. And there appeared to them tongues as of fire distributing themselves, and they rested on each of them. And they were filled with the Holy Spirit and began to speak with other tongues, as the Spirit was giving them utterance.* Acts 2:1-4

*rose again, even so God will bring with Him those who have fallen asleep in Jesus. For this we say to you by the word of the Lord, that we who are alive and remain until the coming of the Lord, will not precede those who have fallen asleep. For the Lord Himself will descend from heaven with a shout, with the voice of the archangel and with the trumpet of God, and the dead in Christ will rise first. Then we who are alive and remain will be caught up together with them in the clouds to meet the Lord in the air, and so we shall always be with the Lord."* 1Thessalonians 4:14-17.

So all those who have died already when the Rapture comes will go first and the living will be caught up in the air with them and with Jesus. Zola Levitt quipped that ...the problem with Christians is, when you plant them in the ground, you know that one day they are going to pop up again. (paraphrased by the author)

The people who come to God during the tribulation and who will then miss the Rapture will not be able to fellowship and worship as the Church has been able to do for almost two thousand years now. They will be persecuted and killed, unless God provides to save them. There will be multitudes that come to God during that time, and many if not most will be killed by the Anti-Christ and his agents. The persecution will be intense, but the rewards great. The multitudes of those killed during the Tribulation are mentioned several times in the book of Revelation.[55]

---

[55] The Bible, God through many authors, *When the Lamb broke the fifth seal, I saw underneath the altar the souls of those who had been slain because of the word of God, and because of the testimony which they had maintained; and they cried out with a loud voice, saying, "How long, O Lord, holy and true, will You refrain from judging and avenging our blood on those who dwell on the earth?" And there was given to each of them a white robe; and they were told that they should rest for a little while longer, until the number of their fellow servants and their brethren who were to be killed even as they had been, would be completed also.* Revelation 6:9-11 *After these things I looked, and behold, a great multitude which no one could count, from every nation and all tribes and peoples and tongues, standing before the throne and before the Lamb, clothed in white robes, and palm branches were in their hand; and they cry out with a loud*

Meanwhile, those members of the Church who were raptured will also be in heaven and will participate in a feast and ceremony in which they, as the Bride of Christ will be married to Yeshua.

*"Let us rejoice and be glad and give the glory to Him, for the marriage of the Lamb has come and His bride has made herself ready."* *It was given to her to clothe herself in fine linen, bright and clean; for the fine linen is the righteous acts of the saints.* *Then he said to me, "Write, 'Blessed are those who are invited to the marriage supper of the Lamb.'"* Revelation 19:7-9

This will be a glorious ceremony that will ritually bind everyone who has been in communion with God from the beginning of creation to Yeshua for eternity. Many will be there who lived before the Age of Grace, many will be there from the Church Age, but all will be bound to Yeshua.

---

*voice, saying, "Salvation to our God who sits on the throne, and to the Lamb.".…And he said to me, "These are the ones who come out of the great tribulation, and they have washed their robes and made them white in the blood of the Lamb. For this reason, they are before the throne of God; and they serve Him day and night in His temple; and He who sits on the throne will spread His tabernacle over them. They will hunger no longer, nor thirst anymore; nor will the sun beat down on them, nor any heat; for the Lamb in the center of the throne will be their shepherd, and will guide them to springs of the water of life; and God will wipe every tear from their eyes." Revelation 7:9-10, 14-17 Here is the perseverance of the saints who keep the commandments of God and their faith in Jesus. And I heard a voice from heaven, saying, "Write, 'Blessed are the dead who die in the Lord from now on!'" "Yes," says the Spirit, "so that they may rest from their labors for their deeds follow with them." Revelation 14:12-13*

# CHAPTER 8

# The World Kingdom

The governments of the world are going to come together at some point in the future and form an overarching government for the entire world. The Humanist Manifesto clearly calls for the formation of this entity. Its twelfth principle states, "We deplore the division of humankind on nationalistic grounds. We have reached a turning point in human history where the best option is to *transcend the limits of national sovereignty* and to move toward the building of a world community in which all sectors of the human family can participate. Thus we look to the development of a system of world law and a world order based upon transnational federal government."[56]

Daniel, the prophet, saw this government in one of his visions.

*"After this I kept looking in the night visions, and behold, a fourth beast, dreadful and terrifying and extremely strong; and it had large iron teeth. It devoured and crushed and trampled down the remainder with its feet; and it was different from all the beasts that were before it, and it had ten horns."* Daniel 7:7

---

[56] Humanist Manifesto II, ed. Paul Kurtz, Prometheus Books, 1973

*"Then I desired to know the exact meaning of the fourth beast, which was different from all the others, exceedingly dreadful, with its teeth of iron and its claws of bronze, and which devoured, crushed and trampled down the remainder with its feet, and the meaning of the ten horns that were on its head and the other horn which came up, and before which three of them fell, namely, that horn which had eyes and a mouth uttering great boasts and which was larger in appearance than its associates...Thus he said, 'the fourth beast will be a fourth kingdom on the earth, which will be different from all the other kingdoms and will devour the whole earth and tread it down and crush it.'"* Daniel 7:19-20,23

This kingdom mentioned in the vision above has traditionally been interpreted as the Roman Empire. But Daniel had another vision about Kingdoms that reflects on the above.

The diviners and other wise men of the king's staff were called before King Nebuchadnezzar to interpret a dream that troubled the king. However, the king would not reveal the dream. He ordered his wise men to tell him what he dreamed and then what the dream meant. No one there could do that, and Nebuchadnezzar ordered all of the kingdom's wise men to be killed. When the captain of the army came to get Daniel to kill him, Daniel asked for another day since he did not know all of this was happening. He was given a vision by God that revealed the dream and its interpretation. When he went in to the king and told him the dream and its interpretation, he was elevated to a high position, and the slaughter of all the wise men was stopped.

Daniel informed Nebuchadnezzar that he had dreamed "what will take place in the latter days." There was a large statue of a man, whose head was
*"made of fine gold, its breast and arms of silver, its belly and its thighs of bronze, its legs of iron, its feet partly of iron and partly of clay. ...a stone was cut out without hands, and it struck*

*the statue on its feet of iron and clay and crushed them."*
Daniel 2:32-34

The interpretation of the dream was given to Daniel and he related it to the King. He told the king,

*"You are the head of gold* (Babylon).
*After you there will arise another kingdom inferior to you* (Medo-Persia), *then another third kingdom of bronze, which will rule over all the earth* (Greece).
*Then there will be a fourth kingdom as strong as iron* (Rome); *inasmuch as iron crushes and shatters all things, so, like iron that breaks in pieces, it will crush and break all these in pieces. As the toes of the feet were partly of iron and partly of pottery, so some of the kingdom will be strong and part of it will be brittle.*
*In the days of those kings the God of heaven will set up a kingdom which will never be destroyed, and that kingdom will not be left for another people; it will crush and put an end to all these kingdoms, but it will itself endure forever.*
*Inasmuch as you saw that a stone was cut out of the mountain without hands and that it crushed the iron, the bronze, the clay, the silver and the gold, the great God has made known to the king what will take place in the future."* Daniel 2:38-42, 44-45.

So God provided Daniel with the prophecy of the future kingdoms arising over the ensuing 300 years, but also a look at the distant World Kingdom. The Anti-Christ will come from a new Roman Empire, likely encompassing the current European states and many of the Mediterranean powers. In another vision, Daniel saw four beasts coming up out of the seas. The first three beasts represented Babylon, Persia-Media, and Greece, corresponding to the vision of the statue discussed previously. The fourth beast was the most powerful of the four, and the most frightening for Daniel. It represented the Roman kingdom, but there were ten horns on the head of the beast. While he was watching, *"another horn a little one, came up among them, and three of the first horns were pulled out by the roots before it; and behold, this horn possessed eyes like the eyes of a man and a mouth uttering great boasts."* Daniel 7:8

Daniel was given the following explanation by an angel:

*"Then I desired to know the exact meaning of the fourth beast, which was different from all the others, exceedingly dreadful, with its teeth of iron and its claws of bronze, and which devoured, crushed and trampled down the remainder with its feet,*
*and the meaning of the ten horns that were on its head and the other horn which came up, and before which three of them fell, namely, that horn which had eyes and a mouth uttering great boasts and which was larger in appearance than its associates.*
*I kept looking, and that horn was waging war with the saints and overpowering them*
*until the Ancient of Days came and judgment was passed in favor of the saints of the Highest One, and the time arrived when the saints took possession of the kingdom."* Daniel 7:19-22

The imagery above is of the World Kingdom headed up by the large horn, whom we call the Anti-Christ. He will use the resources available through this world kingdom to oppress any who believe and follow God. And he will be very successful until the awful Day of The Lord when judgment comes upon him and all who are in rebellion against God.

The angel continued to explain to Daniel,
*"The fourth beast will be a fourth kingdom on the earth, which will be different from all the other kingdoms and will devour the whole earth and tread it down and crush it.*
*As for the ten horns, out of this kingdom ten kings will arise; and another will arise after them, and he will be different from the previous ones and will subdue three kings."* Daniel 7:23-24

The World Kingdom is described here and the ascension of the Anti-Christ described to Daniel. The angel then speaks to the abominations of the Anti-Christ.

*"He will speak out against the Most High and wear down the saints of the Highest One, and he will intend to make alterations in times and in law; and they will be given into his hand for a time, times, and half a time."* Daniel 7:25

However, God's judgment will come upon both the World Kingdom and the Anti-Christ.

*"But the court will sit for judgment, and his dominion will be taken away, annihilated and destroyed forever. Then the sovereignty, the dominion and the greatness of all kingdoms under the whole heaven will be given to the people of the saints of the Highest One; His kingdom will be an everlasting kingdom, and all the dominions will serve and obey Him."* Daniel 7:26-27

The battle of Armageddon is hinted at here, and the final outcome clearly stated. Jesus will defeat the Anti-Christ and his armies from all over the world. Our Lord will establish a kingdom that will be transitional for a thousand years, and then for eternity.

The new World Kingdom will have ten kings, as the statue in Daniel's vision had ten toes mixed with iron and clay. The ten toes were crushed and destroyed by the large stone that represented God's kingdom. The action of crushing the toes represents the coming battle between Jesus and the Anti-Christ and his armies.

We encounter the ten kings of the World Government again in the 17th chapter of Revelation. The apostle John is shown a vision of
*"a woman sitting on a scarlet beast, full of blasphemous names, having seven heads and ten horns."* Revelation 17:3

While the main emphasis of this vision is about the woman, there is an explanation by an angel about the beast and the ten horns. The beast has seven heads which are described as seven mountains and ten kings. Often in prophecy, a mountain is synonymous with a kingdom, and a king is also symbolic of a kingdom. So prophecy expositors have long looked for a coming government composed of seven sections and headed by ten rulers. The angel also enigmatically equates the World Government with the Anti-Christ:

*"The beast which was and is not, is himself also an eighth and is one of the seven, and he goes to destruction."* Revelation 17:11

The Anti-Christ is synonymous with the World Government, indicating he will rule the World Government during the last 3 ½ years of the Tribulation with total power.

The angel then says,
*"The ten horns which you saw are ten kings who have not yet received a kingdom, but they receive authority as kings with the beast for one hour.*
*These have one purpose, and they give their power and authority to the beast."* Revelation 17:12-13

These ten kings seem to act as a unit instead of individual sovereigns. Scriptures suggest that they will be a council of administrators who serve the Anti-Christ. Perhaps they have been elected or appointed from different parts of the world, but cannot govern without the permission of the Anti-Christ. This would again point to the absolute power of the Anti-Christ in the later part of the Tribulation.

The push for a world government began in the 1970s in force, and has been moving in the background, mostly unreported. The objectives of those who are pushing this agenda are clear, and yet, most people in the world are unaware of them. They are public, and are being used by the United Nations and government leaders around the world to "lead" the world in this direction.

*The Humanist Manifesto* of 1973 called for the building of a world community. Also in the late 1960s, the Club of Rome was founded by very prestigious people from around the world. They have been driving the agenda to reduce the world's population and to change the world economy. They have been working through UN committees and NGOs to change the world perspective.

Previously, mankind had thought that the world would continue to get better for people as we learned more about scientific principles and invented more things to help make our lives easier. However, the Club of Rome and its affiliates have changed that outlook. One of their founders explained their strategy,

*"The common enemy of humanity is man. In searching for a new enemy to unite us, we came up with the idea that pollution, the threat of global warming, water shortages, famine and the like would fit the bill. All these dangers are caused by human intervention, and it is only through changed attitudes and behavior that they can be overcome. The real enemy then, is humanity itself."[57]*

The environmental movement which started as people wanting to care for our world and its resources, as commanded by God to Adam, has been high-jacked by elitists who want to push their own agenda.

Further excerpts from the Club's reports and organizations are as follows:

*We support the development of sustainable, decentralized, that is local, high-tech production, combined with local use of*

---

[57] "Aurelio Peccei." AZQuotes.com. Wind and Fly LTD, 2018. 30 July 2018. https://www.azquotes.com/author/46173-Aurelio_Peccei

*local resources. and the redesign of our monetary system according to a fourfold model: 1) economy of gifting (a basic matriarchal feature), 2) **counter-trade (barter) economy**, 3) complementary local monetary systems for regional trade, and 4) **unified currency** (for example called "terra") for interregional and global trade. In our eyes compound interest has to be abolished. **Also the concept of "owning" land must be reconsidered**."*
http://www.worldshiftnetwork.org/action/subsistence.html

"*We support the transition from today's parliamentary democratic systems to participative democratic civil societies all over the world, which are **no longer ruled by politicians, but wisely administered by wisdom-educated professionals**, based on the fundaments of egalitarian consensus principles. In a participative civil society the common guidelines are maintained by parliaments of prudent delegates, who don't possess political power, but present and negotiate the will of their **mandating regions** instead.*

If you read the above statements carefully you understand that they recommend local bartering and use of a "world-wide" currency. They also would/will prohibit personal ownership, thereby instituting communism run by the Elites. Note the part about delegates who don't possess political power but represent their "Regions."

As you consider those delegates, think about the ten kings who have not received a kingdom and give their power and authority to the beast.

In their 1974 report, *Mankind at the Turning Point*, the Club of Rome authors wrote, "*Cooperation by definition connotes interdependence. Increasing interdependence between nations and regions must then translate as a **decrease in independence**. Nations cannot be interdependent without each of them giving up some of, or at least acknowledging limits to, its own independence.*"

152

*"Now is the time to draw up a **master plan for organic sustainable growth and world development based on global allocation of all finite resources and a new global economic system.** Ten or twenty years from today it will probably be too late..."*

The book recommended dividing the world into ten regions as follows:

Region 1:  The U.S.A. and Canada,
Region 2:  Western Europe, Scandinavia, and Turkey,
Region 3:  Japan,
Region 4:  Australia and South Africa,
Region 5:  Russia and Eastern Europe,
Region 6:  South and Central America,
Region 7:  North Africa and the Middle East,
Region 8:  Central Africa,
Region 9:  India and Southeast Asia,
Region 10: China

This could be the source of the ten kings prophesied in Daniel and Revelation.  The administrators from each region could then be

*..."ten kings who have not yet received a kingdom, but they receive authority as kings with the beast for one hour.*

*These have one purpose, and they give their power and authority to the beast."* <u>Revelation 17:12-13</u>

The most strident of the people who are calling for change are those people who call themselves "Gaians." Believers in Gaia claim that the earth is a sentient super-being, an ancient goddess spirit, deserving of worship and reverence. Dr. James Lovelock, who holds degrees in medicine, chemistry and physics is one of the most prominent and influential Gaians.  He wrote the following in regard to global warming:

*"Just as the human body uses a fever to fight off an infection, Gaia is raising Her temperature to expel a harmful parasite – humans. Unless humans renounce their destructive ways and rejoin the diverse community of living beings in Gaia's*

*loving embrace then Gaia will be forced to act in order to secure Her supreme reign."*

Thus Gaians consider humans to be parasites on their Earth Goddess. Therefore the answer to global warming, water shortages, famine, etc. (you pick your favorite world catastrophe) is depopulating the world and changing the forms of government.

Also we see people today who are calling for a World Government to move humanity forward. Many people now refer to themselves as world citizens, and are pushing to remove all national borders.[58]

We are seeing people who are calling for a single currency in the world. The European nations have come together to form the European Union with its own currency, the euro. The movement is already in progress to diminish national interests and have everyone begin to think more about "global" interests. In 2008, the presidential candidate who would become the President of the United States, Barack Obama, made a speech in Berlin, in which he called himself a "citizen of the world". Many have worried that this globalist philosophy will continue to attract people who think that it will lead to world peace and prosperity.

Connected to this movement is the push for a "money-less" society. This movement would do away with cash altogether and require credit or debit cards to do business transactions. The problem of course is that all transactions would be available for audit or review by computer by anyone who has access to those records. During the Tribulation period, no one will be able to buy or sell without a microchip or "mark" on their forearm or forehead. The book of Revelations describes this while describing the "Prophet", the Anti-Christ's right hand man.

---

[58] www.worldcitizens.org

*"And he causes all, the small and the great, and the rich and the poor, and the free men and the slaves, to be given a mark on the right hand or on their forehead,*

*and he provides that no one will be able to buy or to sell, except the one who has the mark, either the name of the beast or the number of his name.*

*Here is wisdom. Let him who has understanding calculate the number of the beast, for the number is that of a man; and his number is six hundred and sixty-six."* <u>Revelation 13:16-18</u>

By prohibiting the use of cash, governments could easily identify and require a special identification process before any business transaction could take place. So those who refuse to take the mark will have much difficulty in obtaining food, energy, or housing. No one would be able to hide or stash money away, because cash money would be worthless. We have all seen business establishments that require credit or debit cards with their "No Cash Please" signs. This government would have all of the power to refuse services to anyone without their special identification.

When the Anti-Christ assumes complete command of the World Government, it will become more oppressive against anyone who resists the new rules and laws. Those people who refuse to take the "Mark of the Beast" will be thrown in prison and executed as the Tribulation progresses in time.

# CHAPTER 9

# The Anti-Christ: The Man of Lawlessness

The man who will come to prominence as the world's leader is called the Anti-Christ (or more correctly translated as the PseudoChrist) by the prophets and the apostles.  He is mentioned in <u>Daniel 7:8, 20-21,24; 9:26-27</u>; and <u>11:36-45</u>, <u>2 Thessalonians 2:1-12</u>, <u>1 John 2:18, Revelation 6:1-2; 13:1-10; 16:13-16; 19:19-20</u>.  Paul says that the apostasy will come first, and then the

*"...man of lawlessness will be revealed, the son of destruction, who opposes and exalts himself above every so-called god or object of worship, so that he takes his seat in the temple of God, displaying himself as being God."* <u>2 Thessalonians 2:3-4</u>

Paul goes on to describe the times and circumstances of the Anti-Christ:

*"For the mystery of lawlessness is already at work; only he who now restrains will do so until he is taken out of the way.*

*Then that lawless one will be revealed whom the Lord will slay with the breath of His mouth and bring to an end by the appearance of His coming;*

*that is, the one whose coming is in accord with the activity of Satan, with all power and signs and false wonders,*

*and with all the deception of wickedness for those who perish, because they did not receive the love of the truth so as to be saved."* 2 Thessalonians 2:7-10

Exactly who it is who is restraining lawlessness is not clearly revealed. The most likely restrainer would be the Holy Spirit. As the world grows darker, and fewer human beings are praying for God's protection, will the Holy Spirit withdraw, leaving us to our human natures? This question of how prayer works for a community, a state, or a nation may be the answer about the rise of lawlessness. One analogy might come from veterinarian medicine. If 80% or more of a herd of animals is vaccinated against a certain viral disease, the chances of <u>any</u> member of that herd becoming ill with that particular disease is reduced tremendously. Likewise, as fewer members of a community are in communion with God, does His protection of that <u>entire</u> community decrease? This certainly could be one explanation of the increasing lawlessness. (However, concerning individuals, we know that when a Christian continues in communion (prayer) with God, and totally submits his/her will to God's will, then God will use that life for His own purposes.)

The Holy Spirit will most likely partially withdraw with the Church when She is raptured. Once the Bride of Christ (the Church) is off of the earth, the great Arch-angel Michael will throw Satan and his followers out of heaven and on to the earth. Satan's power will be increased and the Holy Spirit will partially withdraw, increasing the chaos on earth as people try to live without any semblance of truth to grasp. The Holy Spirit will continue to work on Earth as in the days before Christ's crucifixion and resurrection. Multitudes of people will be drawn to Christ during that time.

Paul then says that as lawlessness increases, the Anti-Christ will be revealed. What will he be like? Daniel implies that he will come from the New Roman Empire, or at least that is how many interpret Daniel 9:26 that says *"...and the people of the prince who is to come will destroy the city and the sanctuary."* Since the Roman army destroyed the second temple in 70 A.D., the assumption is that the "prince to come" will also be from the Roman Empire.

Revelation 13:1-10 also describes the Anti-Christ. Verse 2 stating that *"... (he) was like a leopard, and his feet were like those of a bear, and his mouth like the mouth of a lion."* These represent 3 of the four empires that Daniel saw coming before the Kingdom of God came to earth (Daniel 7). The leopard was Greece, the bear was the Medo-Persian Empire, and the lion was Babylon. The fourth empire was the Roman Empire, incorporating the previous three empires. Thus the Anti-Christ is seen by John as coming from this New Roman confederation centered around the Mediterranean Sea.

At first he will represent a leader who promises peace (Daniel 9:27; *"And he will make a firm covenant with the many."*) He is seen by many to be a very charismatic person, who talks peace and comfort, but plots a course to increase his own power. As his power grows, he begins to wage war against others, breaking the peace that he has engineered up until then.

Daniel 11:40-45 talks about the Anti-Christ waging war against the "King of the South", most probably Egypt. Isaiah 19:4 states, *"I will deliver the Egyptians in the hand of a cruel master, and a mighty king will rule over them."* This is just before the second coming of the Lord, and probably represents the battle between the Egyptian king (King of the South), who is called the cruel master, and the Anti-Christ, called here a mighty king.  The Anti-Christ will then move into Israel and set up his camp between Jerusalem and the sea.  At some point, the Anti-Christ will receive a deadly wound, either in battle or an assassination.  He will be dead for several days, and in a counterfeit of the real Resurrection of Jesus, Satan will appear bring the Anti-Christ back from the dead.

Needless to say, this will impress many of those who do not accept God, and many will follow the Anti-Christ. Halfway into the 7-year Tribulation, he, as head of the World Government, will declare himself god, and set up an idol of himself in the Temple in Jerusalem.  He will raise a large army from these countries which have allied into this Government, and will continually increase his power.

In the seventh chapter of Daniel, the Anti-Christ is said to destroy three of the ten kings, which represent the leaders of ten areas of the world under this single government.

*"While I was contemplating the horns, behold, another horn, a little one, came up among them, and three of the first horns were pulled out by the roots before it; and behold, this horn possessed eyes like the eyes of a man and mouth uttering great boasts.*

*And the meaning of the ten horns that were on its head and the other horn which came up, and before which three of them fell, namely, that horn which had eyes and a mouth uttering great boasts and which was larger in appearance than its associates. I kept looking, and that horn was waging war with the saints and overpowering them*

*...As for the ten horns, out of this kingdom ten kings will arise; and another will arise after them, and he will be different from the previous ones and will subdue three kings."* Daniel 7:8, 20-21, 24

These may be the "King of the South" as mentioned above, and possibly the "King of the East" as mentioned in Daniel 11:44 *"But rumors from the East and the North will disturb him, and he will go forth with great wrath to destroy and annihilate many".* After leaving Egypt and moving into the Holy Land, he will wage war against Jerusalem.

*"Behold, I am going to make Jerusalem a cup that causes reeling to all the peoples around; and when the siege is against Jerusalem, it will also be against Judah. It will come about in that day that I will make Jerusalem a heavy stone for all the peoples; all who lift it will be severely injured. And all the nations of the earth will be gathered against it."* Zechariah 12:2-3

His forces will capture the city. *"For I will gather all the nations against Jerusalem to battle, and the city will be captured, the houses plundered, the women ravished and half of the city exiled, but the rest of the people will not be cut off from the city."* Zechariah14:2

Once that happens, our Lord Jesus will come back and set His feet on the Mount of Olives and decimate the Anti-Christ's army.

*"Then the Lord will go forth and fight against those nations, as when He fights on a day of battle. In that day His feet will stand on the Mount of Olives, which is in front of Jerusalem on the east; and the Mount of Olives will be split in its middle from east to west by a very large valley, so that half of the mountain will move toward the north and the other half toward the south*

*...Now this is the plague with which the Lord will strike all the peoples who have gone to war against Jerusalem; their flesh will rot while they stand on their feet, and their eyes will rot in their sockets, and their tongue will rot in their mouth."* Zechariah 14:3-4, 12

The Anti-Christ and his False Prophet will then be thrown into the fiery lake we refer to as Hell forever.

*"And I saw heaven opened, and behold, a white horse, and He who sat on it is called Faithful and True, and in righteousness*

*He judges and wages war. His eyes are a flame of fire, and on His head are many diadems; and He has a name written on Him which no one knows except Himself. He is clothed with a robe dipped in blood, and His name is called The Word of God.*

*And the armies which are in heaven, clothed in fine linen, white and clean, were following Him on white horses. From His mouth comes a sharp sword, so that with it He may strike down the nations, and He will rule them with a rod of iron; and He treads the wine press of the fierce wrath of God, the Almighty. And on His robe and on His thigh He has a name written, "King of Kings, And Lord of Lords."*

*Then I saw an angel standing in the sun, and he cried out with a loud voice, saying to all the birds which fly in midheaven, "Come, assemble for the great supper of God, so that you may eat the flesh of kings and the flesh of commanders and the flesh of mighty men and flesh of horses and of those who sit on them, and the flesh of all men, both free men and slaves, and small and great."*

*And I saw the beast and kings of the earth and their armies assembled to make war against Him who sat on the horse and against His army. And the beast was seized, and with him the false prophet who performed the signs in his presence, by which he deceived those who had received the mark of the beast and those who worshiped his image; these two were thrown alive into the lake of fire which burns with brimstone.*

*And the rest were killed with the sword which came from the mouth of Him who sat on the horse, and all the birds were filled with their flesh."* <u>Revelation 19:11-21</u>

Thus the Anti-Christ's apparent invincibility will be shown for the sham it is, and Jesus will establish the Millennial Kingdom.

*"Then I saw thrones, and they sat on them, and judgment was given to them. And I saw the souls of those who had been beheaded because of their testimony of Jesus and because of the word of God, and those who had not worshiped the beast or his*

image, and had not received the mark on their forehead and on their hand; and they came to life and reigned with Christ for a thousand years." Revelation 20:4

Isaiah also saw the downfall of the Anti-Christ:

"The Lord has broken the staff of the wicked, the scepter of rulers which subdued the nations in anger with unrestrained persecution." Isaiah 14:5-6

"Sheol from beneath is excited over you to meet you when you come; it arouses for you the spirits of the dead, all the leaders of the earth; it raises all the kings of the nations from their thrones. They will all respond and say to you, 'Even you have been made weak as we, you have become like us. Your pomp and the music of your harps have been brought down to Sheol; maggots are spread out as your bed beneath you and worms are your covering." Isaiah 14:9-11

"Those who see you will gaze at you, they will ponder over you, saying, 'Is this the man who made the earth tremble, who shook kingdoms, who made the world like a wilderness and overthrew its cities, who did not allow his prisoners to go home?'" Isaiah 14:16-17

"But you have been cast out of your tomb like a rejected branch, clothed with the slain who are pierced with a sword, who go down to the stones of the pit like a trampled corpse." Isaiah 14:19

The Anti-Christ will rise to be the most powerful, and the most ruthless, man who ever lived. But in the end, he will be quickly dispatched to Hell by the true Sovereign of the world, Jesus.

# CHAPTER 10

# The World Religion
# &
# The False Prophet

Prior to the Tribulation, and through the first 3 ½ years of the Tribulation, the world's religions will begin to coalesce together in a great ecumenical melting pot to form a religion of inclusivity. Much like universalism of today, everyone will be allowed to worship the god of their desires. The apostate Christian Church will lead in bringing everyone together, and will set up rituals suitable for everyone.

As the mainstream Christian denominations strive for ecumenism and inclusivity, they will "put aside their differences" and begin to fuse into a large global church. The Roman Catholic Church will most likely lead the process and ensure that the Pope remains the primary Christian leader. Lutherans, Anglicans, Methodists, Presbyterians and other denominations will join the process to bring more people back into their empty buildings. The Western Church will then reconcile with the Eastern Orthodox churches and become a world-wide "Christian" church.

This new ecumenical church will begin allowing people of "other" faiths to worship with them, and will probably begin to change their own beliefs to meet the "needs" of those other faiths.

The exception will be religious Jews and "fundamentalist" Christians, who will refuse to acknowledge any other gods than the living God. They will initially be scorned and mocked and cajoled to come into the new church, but later the consequences will be much worse.

Dr. Robert Muller, who died in 2010, was the Assistant Secretary-General of the United Nations for many years. He worked on many committees and fostered the establishment of many of the U.N.'s organizations. He was the author of the concept of a United Religions of the World.

*"My great personal dream is to forge a tremendous alliance between all religions and spiritual groups, and the UN. We desperately need a United Religions Organization to bring reconciliation, unity and peace to all the peoples of our world."*

His idea has continued to gather converts. Today there is an organization called the United Religions Initiative with the stated goal to *"promote enduring, daily interfaith cooperation, to end religiously motivated violence and to create cultures of peace, justice and healing for the Earth and all living beings."* These Global Religion baby steps will no doubt lead to the One-World Religion.

The Roman Catholic Church, since the 1980s, has been moving toward reconciliation with Protestants and other religions. The main goal seems an attempt to bring more people into the Catholic Church. In 1994, a document entitled "Evangelicals and Catholics Together: The Christian Mission in the 3rd Millennium" was signed by leading American evangelicals and Catholics. It has been applauded by many as a first step in re-uniting "the Church." Part of the "reconciliation" between Protestants and Catholics has been the agreement to stop trying to proselytize each other's members. Evangelicals feel that anyone being taught about Jesus should be saved, and therefore do not object to people entering the Catholic Church. However, for the Catholics, it is a means to increase their membership. Father Tom Forrest has led the Catholic evangelical movement. Here is part of his explanation of Catholic evangelism:

"Our job is to make people as richly and as fully Christian as we can make them by bringing them into the Catholic Church. So evangelization is never fully successful, it's only partial, until the convert is made a member of Christ's body by being led into the [Catholic] Church.

No, you don't just invite someone to become a Christian, you invite them to become Catholics...Why would this be so important? First of all, there are seven sacraments, and the Catholic Church has all seven...On our altars we have the body of Christ; we drink the blood of Christ. Jesus is alive on our altars, as offering...We become one with Christ in the Eucharist."[59]

But Catholics are not just interested in Protestants. Sri Chinmoy, known as the "guru of the United Nations" was apparently considered a friend of Pope John Paul II, who told him, "Special blessings to you...and to your members. We shall continue together." Pope Paul VI told Chinmoy, "The Hindu life and the Christian life shall go together. Your message and my message are the same."[60] So neither Pope had a problem with Hinduism. Pope John Paul II said, "the Catholic Church ...wants to establish positive and cooperative

---

[59] "Roman Catholic Doubletalk at Indianapolis '90," *Foundation*, July-Aug. 1990, excerpts from talk by Fr. Tom Forrest to the Roman Catholic Saturday morning training session.

[60] A Woman Rides the Beast, Dave Hunt, Harvest House Publishers, 1994; page 417.

relations with...various faiths in view of a mutual enrichment."[61]  Pope John Paul II also asked Christians and Muslims to meet each other in faith in the one God, as if the Living God and Allah were the same.  He thanked Shintoists and Buddhists in Tokyo for "(seeing) a divine presence in each human being."

This amalgamation of differing faiths will continue to grow until it becomes a unifying World Religion.  The apostle John was shocked when the Lord showed him a vision of the apostate church which he recorded in the book of Revelation.

He was shown the vision of a woman riding on a terrible beast.

*"Then one of the seven angels who had the seven bowls came and spoke with me, saying, 'Come here, I will show the judgment of the great harlot who sits on many waters,*

*With whom the kings of the earth committed acts of immorality, and those who dwell on the earth were made drunk with the wine of her immorality.'*

*And he carried me away in the Spirit into a wilderness;* **and I saw a woman sitting on a scarlet beast, full of blasphemous names, having seven heads and ten horns.**

**The woman was clothed in purple and scarlet, and adorned with gold and precious stones and pearls, having in her hand a gold cup full of abominations and of the unclean things of her immorality,**

*And on her forehead a name was written, a mystery,* "BABYLON THE GREAT, THE MOTHER OF HARLOTS AND OF THE ABOMINATIONS OF THE EARTH."

*And* **I saw the woman drunk with the blood of the saints, and with the blood of the witnesses of Jesus.** *When I saw her, I was astonished."* Revelation 17:1-6

---

[61] A Woman Rides the Beast, Dave Hunt, Harvest House Publishers, 1994, page 418.

John was astonished because the woman represented the Church and called itself "Christian" and yet was full of immorality. This End Times Church will be responsible for the death of more Christians than the ancient Roman Empire, Muslims, Hindus and other opponents of the religion combined. Those evangelical Christians who refuse to accept the inclusivity of the new church will be ostracized at first, mocked and scorned next, and finally arrested and detained.

This was John's third vision of this beast with seven heads and ten horns. First the seven-headed beast represented Satan himself:

"*Then another sign appeared in heaven: and behold, a great red dragon having seven heads and ten horns, and on his heads were seven diadems.*" Revelation 12:3

Then another beast (not a dragon) was seen that represented the Anti-Christ:

"*Then I saw a beast coming up out of the sea, having ten horns and seven heads, and on his horns were ten diadems, and on his heads were blasphemous names.*" Revelation 13:1

But in this vision the emphasis is not on the beast, which has represented Satan, the Anti-Christ, and now the One-World Government, but instead the emphasis is on the woman riding the beast. She is described as a harlot, or prostitute, for committing immorality with the kings of the earth.

The woman is riding the beast that represents the One-World Government and the Anti-Christ. At first she will be like a person riding a horse—trying to control that government and its leaders. The popes from the Middle Ages to the late 1800s certainly did that in almost every nation of Europe. Since no one could get out of Purgatory and into Heaven without the Church's intervention, even kings were afraid to anger the popes. That same kind of influence will probably be the mindset of the church leader(s) in the early stages of the church. The Anti-Christ will let the apostate church bring people into the fold with promises of peace and contentment in the new religion.

But toward the middle of the Tribulation, the government will turn on the church and destroy it.

*"And the ten horns which you saw, and the beast, these will hate the harlot and will make her desolate and naked, and will eat her flesh and will burn her up with fire.*

*For God has put it in their hearts to execute His purpose by having a common purpose, and by giving their kingdom to the beast, until the words of God will be fulfilled."* Revelation 17:16-17

The Anti-Christ and his "Council" will ridicule the church, strip it of all power, and take all of the money that it had collected for their own uses. They apparently will destroy many of the church buildings also, perhaps even burning them.

The "Second Beast," also known as the Prophet, will rise to power in the church, and become the leader. Together with the Anti-Christ, they will begin to change the ideology of the church to recognize the "spiritual" side of the Anti-Christ. Around the mid-point of the Tribulation, the Anti-Christ will suffer a severe wound to his head. He will be pronounced dead, and then amazingly, he will be "healed" through the power of Satan. After that, the people of the world will be easily convinced that the Anti-Christ is indeed a god, and they will begin to worship him. Satan and the Anti-Christ will be "one" as Christ and God the Father are one. In all things, the Anti-Christ will try to counterfeit the reality of Christ.

*"And the beast which I saw was like a leopard, and his feet were like those of a bear, and his mouth like the mouth of a lion. And the dragon gave him his power and his throne and great authority.*

170

*I saw one of his heads as if it had been slain, and his fatal wound was healed and the whole earth was amazed and followed after the beast."* Revelation 13:2-3

The Prophet will then proclaim the Anti-Christ as god, and the World Religion will then resort to a form of Emperor Worship, as in ancient Rome.

*"They worshiped the dragon because he gave his authority to the beast; and they worshiped the beast, saying, 'Who is like the beast, and who is able to wage war with him?'*

*There was given to him a mouth speaking arrogant words and blasphemies; and authority to act for forty-two months was given to him.*

*And he opened his mouth in blasphemies against God, to blaspheme His name and His tabernacle, that is, those who dwell in heaven.*

*It was also given to him to make war with the saints and to overcome them, and authority over every tribe and people and tongue and nation was given to him.*

**All who dwell on the earth will worship him,** *everyone whose name has not been written from the foundation of the world in the book of life of the Lamb who has been slain."*
Revelation 13:4-8

The Prophet will do great miracles through the power of Satan, who will give the Anti-Christ great power. John saw the Prophet as follows:

*"Then I saw another beast coming out of the earth; and he had two horns like a lamb and spoke as a dragon.*

*He exercises all the authority of the first beast in his presence,* **and he makes the earth and those who dwell in it to worship the first beast,** *whose fatal wound was healed.*

*He performs great signs, so that he even makes fires come down out of heaven to the earth in the presence of men.*
Revelation 13:11-13

171

Midway into the Tribulation, the Anti-Christ will go into the Jewish Temple in Jerusalem and declare himself to be god. This is the Abomination of Desolation spoken of in the book of Daniel that Jesus made reference to in His Olivet discourse.

*"Let no one in any way deceive you, for it will not come unless the apostasy comes first, and the man of lawlessness is revealed, the son of destruction,*
*Who opposes and exalts himself above every so-called god or object of worship, so that he takes his seat in the temple of God, displaying himself as being god."* 2 Thessalonians 2:3-4

His Prophet will set up a speaking statue of the Anti-Christ in the temple.
*"And he deceives those who dwell on the earth because of the signs which it was given him to perform in the presence of the beast, telling those who dwell on the earth to make an image to the beast who had the wound of the sword and has come to life.*
*And it was given to him to give breath to the image of the beast, so that the image of the beast would even speak and cause as many as do not worship the image of the beast to be killed."* Revelation 13:14-15

Anyone who does not worship the Anti-Christ and his idol will be killed. Followers of Jesus will have to decide between worshipping Jesus or worshipping the Beast. If they choose to bow down to the Anti-Christ, they will forfeit the salvation they had through Jesus's blood.

Once the Anti-Christ establishes himself as god, the Great Tribulation begins and the terrible Trumpet judgments which devastate a third of the world and mankind begin, followed by the Bowl judgments which wreak havoc on all of the world.

# CHAPTER 11

# The Tribulation

The tribulation of the End Times is mentioned in several places in the Bible. Jesus mentions the Tribulation in the Olivet Discourse verifying that it will occur:

*"For then there will be a great tribulation, such as has not occurred since the beginning of the world until now, nor ever will. Unless those days had been cut short, no life would have been saved; but for the sake of the elect those days will be cut short.* Matthew 24: 21-22

The length of the Tribulation is not entirely clear from biblical references, ranging from 3 ½ years (1260 days using lunar months of 30 days each) to 7 years. The most common interpretation today is that the Tribulation will last 7 years with the first 3 ½ years rather peaceful and the second 3 ½ years of severe conditions. Many call the second half of the 7 years the "Great Tribulation", alluding to the words of Jesus in the Olivet Discourse. The seven year interpretation comes from the book of Daniel, specifically the verses of chapter 9: 24-27. Gabriel was speaking to Daniel, informing him of future events. He told Daniel of seventy "sevens" that will be the time frame of future events. Many call these "sevens" weeks to reduce the confusion of talking about seventy and sevens. The sevens are composed of seven year periods. So the total seventy "weeks" compose 490 years altogether. Gabriel then broke the 490 years into smaller sections. He told Daniel that Jerusalem would be rebuilt in seven "weeks", or 49 years. Then 62 "weeks" later (434 years) Messiah would come and be "cut off". This accounts for 69 of the 70 "weeks" or seven-year periods. The final week, or seven year period, is described in verse 27.

"And **he** will make a firm covenant with the many for one week, but in the middle of the week he will put a stop to sacrifice and grain offering; and on the wing of abominations will come one who makes desolate, even until a complete destruction, one that is decreed, is poured out on the one who makes desolate." Daniel 9:27

Scholars of the Hebrew language state that the "he" described above refers back to the prince noted in verse 26 who will come and destroy the city and the sanctuary. So the interpretation is that the Anti-Christ will be of Roman origins and will make (or confirm) a covenant of peace with Israel, which he will break 3 ½ years into the covenant. Then he will set himself up as god in the temple (The Abomination of Desolation), and the Great Tribulation will begin.

Other interpreters--primarily in the Seventh Day Adventist denomination-- say that the "he" of verse 27 is Jesus Himself. In their interpretation, they say that the covenant mentioned is the New Covenant that Jesus began preaching at the beginning of His ministry on earth. The end of the sacrifice comes 3 ½ years later in the middle of the "week" when Jesus is crucified and sacrifices in the Temple are no longer needed. The end of the "week" in their view then came when Stephen was killed by the Sanhedrin, and the persecution of the Church began in Jerusalem. Believers were dispersed, carrying the Good News with them. The problem with this interpretation is the failure to consider the rest of verse 27 which reveals the abominations and the one who makes desolate, and the complete destruction of the one who makes desolate.

Those who hold to this interpretation state that this relates to the Romans who destroyed the Temple in 70 A.D. But the general of the Roman legions which were surrounding and laying siege to Jerusalem was Vespasian, who left the siege in 69 A.D. and became Emperor of the Roman Empire. He left his son, Titus, to continue the siege as general of the legions. Titus finally broke the siege in 70 A.D. and destroyed the Temple. Titus later became Emperor after his father died. So "complete destruction" was never poured out on them. Also the sacrifices in the temple continued for over 30 years after the death of Jesus until the destruction of the temple. No explanation for these problems are offered by those who put forth this interpretation.

If we accept seven years as the length of the Tribulation, and that it is broken into two halves, with the first half being a trying time, but bearable, and the second half as "hell on earth", we can begin to see what the biblical prophecies say about that period of time.

The "he" described in verse 27 is considered by most expositors as the Anti-Christ. He will bring relative peace to Israel through a new peace plan (firm covenant). However, he will continue to consolidate his power during this time, and will war against three other leaders of the World Government (Daniel 7:8 and 24, as discussed previously). During the first three and a half years, the third Jewish Temple (the Tribulation Temple) will be in use.

The Temple could be built soon after the failed Russo-Iranian attack, if Islam falls apart. If Muslims see that it is God Himself who protects Israel, many might lose their passion for Allah, and the Temple Mount could revert back to Israel.

With no one to defend Islam, the Dome of the Rock could be razed and the new Jewish Temple built.

Another possibility is that the Anti-Christ himself could negotiate a truce between Muslims and Jews in Jerusalem, and allow the temple to be built on an existing area of the Temple Mount without destroying any buildings. Another scenario would be building the Temple near the current Temple Mount, but not on it. Whichever scenario is correct, the Temple will be built. The Anti-Christ will set himself up as god in the temple. So a temple must be there by the halfway point of the seven year Tribulation. Also, the apostle John, in his vision of the Revelation, is asked to measure the temple:

*"Then there was given me a measuring rod like a staff; and someone said, 'Get up and measure the temple of God and the altar, and those who worship in it.*

*Leave out the court which is outside the temple and do not measure it, for it has been given to the nations; and they will tread under foot the holy city for forty-two months.'"* <u>Revelation 11: 1-2</u>

Today, men are being trained to be the priests, and the instruments and altar have already been manufactured awaiting the building of this temple. It will probably be destroyed partially or fully during the Battle of Jerusalem between the forces of the Anti-Christ and the Jewish defenders of the city.

Also during this first 3 ½ years, the Two Witnesses described in Revelation will serve as witnesses for God in Jerusalem.

*"And I will grant authority to my two witnesses, and they will prophesy for twelve hundred and sixty days, clothed in sackcloth.*
*These are the two olive trees and the two lampstands that stand*

*before the Lord of the earth.* [62]

*And if anyone wants to harm them, fire flows out of their mouth and devours their enemies; so if anyone wants to harm them, he must be killed in this way.*

*These have the power to shut up the sky, so that rain will not fall during the days of their prophesying; and they have power over the waters to turn them into blood, and to strike the earth with every plague, as often as they desire.*

*When they have finished their testimony, the beast that comes up out of the abyss will make war with them, and overcome them and kill them.*

*And their dead bodies will lie in the street of the great city which mystically is called Sodom and Egypt, where also their Lord was crucified.*

*Those from the peoples and tribes and tongues and nations will look at their dead bodies for three and a half days, and will not permit their dead bodies to be laid in a tomb.*

*And those who dwell on the earth will rejoice over them and celebrate; and they will send gifts to one another, because these two prophets tormented those who dwell on the earth.*

*But after the three and a half days, the breath of life from God came into them, and they stood on their feet; and great fear fell upon those who were watching them.*

*And they heard a loud voice from heaven saying to them, "Come up here." Then they went up into heaven in the cloud, and their enemies watched them."* Revelation 11:3-12

Zola Levitt and other messianic Jewish Christians have noted that the 144,000 saints described in Chapter 14 of Revelation will be the faithful Jews described in Revelation

---

[62] The Bible, God through multiple authors; *"...also two olive trees by it, one on the right side of the bowl and the other on its left side." Then I said to the angel who was speaking with me saying, "What are these, my lord?"* Zechariah 4:3-4; *Then I said to him, "What are these two olive trees on the right of the lampstand and on its left?" And I answered the second time and said to him, "What are the two olive branches which are beside the two golden pipes, which empty the golden oil from themselves?" . Then he said, "These are the two anointed ones who are standing by the Lord of the whole earth."* Zechariah 4:11-14

7:4-8.[63]/[64] They postulate that after the Church is raptured off the earth, the only ones left on earth who will have knowledge of God will be Jews. Scripture says that these 144,000 men will *"follow the Lamb wherever He goes...and no lie was found in their mouth; they are blameless."*[65] These men will be God's evangelists during the Tribulation, proclaiming Yeshua throughout Israel and the world, bringing untold multitudes to salvation. They will undoubtedly be severely abused by the Anti-Christ and his men. Those who remain of the 144,000 preachers and all of the believers who are still alive at the end of the Tribulation will be judged as sheep and will be on Yeshua's right hand side at the Judgment of the Nations following Yeshua's return to earth.

---

[63] The Bible, God through multiple authors; *And I saw another angel ascending from the rising of the sun, having the seal of the living God; and he cried out with a loud voice to the four angels to whom it was granted to harm the earth and the sea, saying, "Do not harm the earth or the sea or the trees until we have sealed the bondservants of our God on their foreheads." And I heard the number of those who were sealed, one hundred and forty-four thousand sealed from every tribe of the sons of Israel: from the tribe of Judah, twelve thousand were sealed, from the tribe of Reuben twelve thousand, from the tribe of Gad twelve thousand, from the tribe of Asher twelve thousand, from the tribe of Naphtali twelve thousand, from the tribe of Manasseh twelve thousand, from the tribe of Simeon twelve thousand, from the tribe of Levi twelve thousand, from the tribe of Issachar twelve thousand, from the tribe of Zebulun twelve thousand, from the tribe of Joseph twelve thousand, from the tribe of Benjamin, twelve thousand were sealed.* Revelation 7:2-8

[64] Coming: The End!, Thomas McCall and Zola Levitt, Zola Levitt Ministries, 1999

[65] The Bible, God through multiple authors: *"Then I looked, and behold, the Lamb was standing on Mount Zion, and with Him one hundred and forty-four thousand, having His name and the name of His Father written on their foreheads. And I heard a voice from heaven, like the sound of many waters and like the sound of loud thunder, and the voice which I heard was like the sound of harpists playing on their harps. And they sang a new song before the throne and before the four living creatures and the elders; and no one could learn the song except the one hundred and forty-four thousand who had been purchased from the earth. These are the ones who have not been defiled with women, for they have kept themselves chaste. These are the ones who follow the Lamb wherever He goes. These have been purchased from among men as first fruits to God and to the Lamb. And no lie was found in their mouth; they are blameless."* Revelation 14:1-5

The Anti-Christ will apparently be wounded, and pronounced dead at the end of this first 3 ½ years, and several days later he will come back to life as a counterfeit of Jesus's resurrection

*"And the beast which I saw was like a leopard, and his feet were like those of a bear, and his mouth like the mouth of a lion. And the dragon gave him his power and his throne and great authority.*
***I saw one of his heads as if it had been slain, and his fatal wound was healed.*** *And the whole earth was amazed and followed after the beast."* Revelation 13:2-3

At that time he will set himself up as a god in the Temple in Jerusalem.
*"...and the man of lawlessness is revealed, the son of destruction, who opposes and exalts himself above every so-called god or object of worship, so **that he takes his seat in the temple of God, displaying himself as being God"*** 2 Thessalonians 2:3b-4;

*"And he will make a firm covenant with the many for one week, but in the middle of the week he will put a stop to sacrifice and grain offering; and on the wing of abominations will come one who makes desolate, even until a complete destruction, one that is decreed, is poured out on the one who makes desolate."* Daniel 9:27

Also during these first 42 months, the Great Apostasy, the world-wide false religion headed by the False Prophet will be promulgated and spread across the world.

*"Then I saw another beast coming up out of the earth; and he had two horns like a lamb and he spoke as a dragon.*
*He exercises all the authority of the first beast in his presence. And he makes the earth and those who dwell in it to worship the first beast, whose fatal wound was healed.*
*He performs great signs, so that he even makes fire come*

*down out of heaven to the earth in the presence of men.*

*And he deceives those who dwell on the earth because of the signs which it was given him to perform in the presence of the beast, telling those who dwell on the earth to make an image to the beast who had the wound of the sword and has come to life.*

*And it was given to him to give breath to the image of the beast, so that the image of the beast would even speak and cause as many as do not worship the image of the beast to be killed."*
Revelation 13:11-15

When the Anti-Christ sets himself up as god after he is resurrected, he will become more aggressive.

*"There was given to him a mouth speaking arrogant words and blasphemies, and authority to act for forty-two months was given to him.*

*And he opened his mouth in blasphemies against God, to blaspheme His name and His tabernacle, that is, those who dwell in heaven.*

*It was also given to him to make war with the saints and to overcome them, and authority over every tribe and people and tongue and nation was given to him.*

*All who dwell on the earth will worship him, everyone whose name has not been written from the foundation of the world in the book of life of the Lamb who has been slain."*
Revelation 13:5-8.

He will then begin to make more demands on his "subjects". All will be required to accept the "Mark of the Beast" in order to be able to buy or sell any product, including food

*"And he causes all, the small and the great, and the rich and the poor, and the free men and the slaves, to be given a mark on the right hand or on their forehead,*

*and he provides that no one will be able to buy or to sell, except the one who has the mark, either the name of the beast or the number of his name."* Revelation 13:16-17

Conditions on earth will deteriorate as the Judgments of God continue. There are three sets of Judgments, seven in each set. These are telescopic, in that the breaking of the seventh Seal sets up the next set of seven judgments called the Seven Trumpets. And the sounding of the seventh Trumpet sets up the third and final set of seven judgments called the Seven Bowls or Vials. The first seven Judgments or Woes, called the seven "Seals" are described in Revelation 6 and probably all occur during the first 3 ½ year period. The second seven Judgments—the Trumpet Judgments—probably will begin either at the end of the first 3 ½ year period or the beginning of the second period—known as the Great Tribulation.

When the seventh Trumpet is blown, the great and awesome "Day of the Lord" begins. This period of time, known as the Day of the Lord, was described by Isaiah:

*"For the Lord of hosts will have a day of reckoning against everyone who is proud and lofty and against everyone who is lifted up, that he may be abased*

*The pride of man will be humbled and the loftiness of men will be abased; and the Lord alone will be exalted n that day, But the idols will completely vanish.*

*Men will go into caves of the rocks and into holes of the ground before the terror of the Lord and the splendor of His majesty, when He arises to make the earth tremble."* Isaiah 2:12, 17-19

And [included in His prophecy against Babylon]

*"Wail, for the day of the Lord is near! It will come as destruction from the Almighty.*

*Therefore all hands will fall limp, and every man's heart will melt.*

*They will be terrified, pains and anguish will take hold of them; they will writhe like a woman in labor, they will look at one another in astonishment, their faces aflame.*

*Behold, the day of the Lord is coming, cruel, with fury and* burning anger, to make the land a desolation; and He will exterminate its sinners from it.

*For the stars of heaven and their constellations will not flash forth their light; the sun will be dark when it rises and the moon will not shed its light.*

*Thus I will punish the world for its evil and the wicked for their iniquity; I will also put an end to the arrogance of the proud and abase the haughtiness of the ruthless.*

*I will make mortal man scarcer than pure gold and mankind than the gold of Ophir.*

*Therefore I will make the heavens tremble, and the earth will be shaken from its place at the fury of the Lord of hosts in the day of His burning anger."* Isaiah 13:6-13

The prophet Joel also foresaw an awesome Day of the Lord:

*"Blow a trumpet in Zion, and sound an alarm on My holy mountain! Let all the inhabitants of the land tremble, for the day of the Lord is coming; surely it is near,*

*A day of darkness and gloom, a day of clouds and thick darkness*

*I will display wonders in the sky and on the earth, blood, fire and columns of smoke.*

*The sun will be turned into darkness and the moon into blood before the great and awesome day of the Lord comes."* Joel 2:1-2a, 30-31

Zechariah described it in the following manner:
*"In that day there will be no light; the luminaries will dwindle.*

*For it will be a unique day which is known to the Lord, neither day nor night, but it will come about that at evening time there will be light."* Zechariah 14:6-7

Will the atmosphere be filled with dust or smoke so that the sun and stars cannot be seen? We do not know the particulars of that time, but even the description of God's fifth Bowl of Wrath states that *"his (Anti-Christ) kingdom became* darkened; and they gnawed their tongues because of pain." Revelation 16:10. So darkness will descend upon the earth in those Last Days.

The last Old Testament prophet, Malachi also saw that Day.

"For behold, the day is coming, burning like a furnace; and all the arrogant and every evildoer will be chaff; and the day that is coming will set them ablaze," says the Lord of hosts, "so that it will leave them neither root nor branch." Malachi 4:1.

Even Paul, writing years before the Revelation of the end times was given to John, knew of that coming Day of the Lord. He wrote of it in his letter to the Thessalonians.

"Now as to the times and the epochs, brethren, you have no need of anything to be written to you.

For you yourselves know full well that the day of the Lord will come just like a thief in the night.

While they are saying, "Peace and safety!" then destruction will come upon them suddenly like labor pains upon a woman with child, and they will not escape." 1Thessalonians 5:1-3

The Day of the Lord is not actually a single day, but an unknown period of time that may be days, weeks, months, or even years long. It will be the time during which God pours out His judgments on unrepentant Mankind. This will be a time when conditions on earth are literally akin to "Hell on Earth". The seven Trumpet Judgments will affect about a third of the world and its inhabitants with each judgment. However, the seven Bowls of Wrath are indeed severe and will affect the entire earth and all its inhabitants. The Bowl Judgments are clear signs of God's judgment on those who remain arrogant and unrepentant. All the water on the earth will be turned to blood and undrinkable. The sun will become much hotter and scorch the earth with unthinkable fierce heat (the ultimate global warming).

*"The fourth angel poured out his bowl upon the sun, and it was given to it to scorch men with fire.*

*Men were scorched with fierce heat; and they blasphemed the name of god who has the power over these plagues, and they did not repent so as to give Him glory."* <u>Revelation 16:8-9</u>

Electricity may no longer be available, so air conditioning might not be an option. The Euphrates and Nile rivers will dry up. Still men will curse God and not repent as noted in Revelation.

*"For they blasphemed the God of heaven because of their pains and their sores; and they did not repent of their deeds."* <u>Revelation 16:11</u>

Finally, there will be an earthquake of previously unheard intensity, which, with the melting of the icecaps, will flood much of the earth and its islands. Huge hailstones will then pommel the earth and its remaining people

*"...and there was a great earthquake, such as there had not been since man came to be upon the earth, so great an earthquake was it, and so mighty*

*...and every island fled away, and the mountains were not found.*

*And huge hailstones, about one hundred pounds each, came down from heaven upon men; and men blasphemed God because of the plague of the hail, because its plague was extremely severe."* <u>Revelation 16:18b,20,21</u>

Sometime after assuming his place as one of the ruling "kings" of the future world kingdom, the Anti-Christ will begin to war against other leaders. It may be during those times that he subdues three of the ten "kings" as noted in Daniel 7. Traditional interpretation concludes that much of Daniel 11 is a description of the Seleucid wars (252-167 B.C.) up to verse 36, which then shifts to the future and describes the Anti-Christ. Certainly verses 2-4 describe the historical events leading up to and including the conquests of Alexander the Great. Verse 4 talks about Alexander's kingdom being divided into 4 parts, which happened upon his death.

"*Behold, three more kings are going to arise in Persia. Then a fourth will gain far more riches than all of them; as soon as he becomes strong through his riches, he will arouse the whole empire against the realm of Greece.*
*And a mighty king will arise, and he will rule with great authority and do as he pleases.*
*But as soon as he has arisen, his kingdom will be broken up and parceled out toward the four points of the compass, though not to his own descendants, nor according to his authority which he wielded, for his sovereignty will be uprooted and given to others besides them.*" Daniel 11:2-4

Then verses 5-20 relate the ongoing wars between the Egyptian kings (Greek general Ptolemy's descendants) and the Syrian kings (Greek general Seleucus' descendants). Verses 21-35 have been thought to describe the persecution of Israel by Antiochus IV Epiphanes, the Syrian king from 175 to 164 B.C.

Verse 36 supposedly then shifts to the future to describe the actions of the Anti-Christ. However, if the Seleucid wars were a type, or foreshadowing of future events, verses 10-45 could describe some of the battles the Anti-Christ will fight in the End Times. What begins as a time of peace when all of the peoples of the world are brought together under the leadership of the charismatic Anti-Christ, becomes a time of unrivaled war and destruction. As the Anti-Christ consolidates power, some of his captains will turn against him. He will receive a wound during a battle that should kill him.

But then the Anti-Christ will then be apparently resurrected from the dead, and begin to promote himself and gather political and military support:

*"...a despicable person will arise, on whom the honor of kingship has not been conferred, but he will come in a time of tranquility and seize the kingdom by intrigue."* <u>Daniel 11:21</u>

Due to his false resurrection, he will gather many followers and will become stronger and stronger.

*"I saw one of his heads as if it had been slain, and his fatal wound was healed. And the whole earth was amazed and followed after the beast; they worshiped the dragon because he gave his authority to the beast; and they worshiped the beast, saying, "Who is like the beast, and who is able to wage war with him?""* <u>Revelation 13:3-4</u>

He will then move into Israel and will set himself up as god in the Temple. He will become very strong militarily and politically, and begin to magnify himself.

*"His armed forces will rise up to desecrate the temple fortress and will abolish the daily sacrifice. Then they will set up the abomination that causes desolation. With flattery he will corrupt those who have violated the covenant, but the people who know their God will firmly resist him.* <u>Daniel 11:31-32</u>

*The king will do as he pleases. He will exalt and magnify himself above every god and will say unheard-of-things against the God of gods. He will be successful until the time of wrath is completed, for what has been determined must take place."* <u>Daniel 11:36</u>

He and the other kings of the world government will then dismantle the apostate church that they had previously supported in order for the people of the world to begin to worship the Anti-Christ.

The False Prophet will now set up a statue of the Anti-Christ and require everyone to worship it and the Anti-Christ.

*"And he deceives those who dwell on the earth because of the signs which it was given him to perform in the presence of the beast, telling those who dwell on the earth to make an image to the beast who had the wound of the sword and has come to life.*

*And it was given to him to give breath to the image of the beast, so that the image of the beast would even speak and cause as many as do not worship the image of the beast to be killed."* Revelation 13:14-15

As conditions on earth continue to deteriorate due to the Judgments of God, some will begin to doubt the Anti-Christ is as powerful as he has portrayed himself to be. The King of the South and two other kings will come together and fight him. He will defeat them and enter Israel.

*"At the end time the king of the South will collide with him, and the king of the North will storm against him with chariots, with horsemen and with many ships; and he will enter countries, overflow them and pass through."* Daniel 11:40

*"He will also enter the Beautiful Land, and many countries will fall; but these will be rescued out of his hand: Edom, Moab and the foremost of the sons of Ammon"* Daniel 11:41

He will then also be the master of Egypt
*"I will deliver the Egyptians into the hand of a cruel master, and a mighty king will rule over them."* Isaiah 19:4, and he will besiege Jerusalem and move his base of operations to Egypt

*"Then he will stretch out his hand against other countries, and the land of Egypt will not escape.*
*But he will gain control over the hidden treasures of gold and silver and over all the precious things of Egypt; and Libyans and Ethiopians will follow at his heels."* Daniel 11:42-43

He will receive news of unrest coming at him from the north and east

*"But rumors from the East and from the North will disturb him, and he will go forth with great wrath to destroy and annihilate many."* Daniel 11:44

187

He will then move his base to a camp in the valley of Jezreel, east of Meggido:

*"He will pitch the tents of his royal pavilion between the seas and the beautiful Holy Mountain; yet he will come to his end, and no one will help him."* Daniel 11:45.

From there he will gather all the nations of the world to fight against the defenders of Jerusalem.

*"And I saw coming out of the mouth of the dragon and out of the mouth of the beast and out of the mouth of the false prophet, three unclean spirits like frogs;*
*for they are spirits of demons, performing signs, which go out to the kings of the whole world, to gather them together for the war of the great day of God, the Almighty."* Revelation16:13-14

The Anti-Christ and his army will overwhelm the Holy City, and exile half of the inhabitants.

*"Behold, I am going to make Jerusalem a cup that causes reeling to all the peoples around; and when the siege is against Jerusalem, it will also be against Judah.*
*It will come about in that day that I will make Jerusalem a heavy stone for all the peoples; all who lift it will be severely injured. And all the nations of the earth will be gathered against it."* Zechariah 12:2-3

*"For I will gather all the nations against Jerusalem to battle, and the city will be captured, the houses plundered, the women ravished and half the city exiled, but the rest of the people will not be cut off from the city."* Zechariah14:2

During this battle of Jerusalem, the third Temple (the Tribulation Temple) apparently will be severely damaged or completely destroyed. The world conditions will be abysmal at that time, as all the water will be exhausted and the heat will be deadly as the seven Bowls of Wrath are poured out on the earth. With no electricity and no personal comforts, people will be brutal and ruthless in dealing with one another.

The stage will be set for the Glorious Appearance.

# CHAPTER 12

# The Second Coming

## THE GLORIOUS APPEARANCE

Jesus is coming back to this earth. This is the assurance from Scripture and from Jesus Himself. Daniel saw ..."*One like a Son of Man coming with the clouds of heaven*", and ..." *to Him was given dominion, glory and a kingdom, that all the peoples, nations and men of every language might serve Him*" <u>Daniel 7:13-14</u>

Jesus said, "*But immediately after the tribulation of those days The Sun Will Be Darkened, and the Moon Will Not Give Its Light, and the Stars Will Fall from the sky, and the powers of the heavens will be shaken. And then the sign of the Son of Man will appear in the sky, and then all the tribes of the earth will mourn, and they will see the Son of Man Coming On the Clouds of The Sky with power and great glory.*" <u>Matthew 24:29-30</u>

As the disciples watched Jesus ascend from the Mount of Olives

*...*"*two men in white clothing stood beside them. They also said, 'Men of Galilee, why do you stand looking into the sky?* **This Jesus, who has been taken up from you into heaven, will come in just the same way as you have watched Him go into heaven.*'"*
Acts 1:10-11

How then will He return?  The apostle John saw

*...*"*heaven opened, and behold, a white horse, and He who sat on it is called Faithful and True, and in righteousness He judges and wages war.*
*...And the armies which are in heaven, clothed in fine linen, white and clean, were following Him on white horses.*"
Revelation 19:11,14

When He returns, the final war, which has been called Armageddon from the Scriptures will begin.  God's Judgments will have reduced the unrepentant survivors to snarling barbarians.  Upon His return, Yeshua will fight several battles, destroying Babylon and all the armies arrayed against Him.  The new city of Babylon, either located at its ancient site in Iraq, or in some other country, will be annihilated immediately.

*"And the kings of the earth, who committed acts of immorality and lived sensuously with her, will weep and lament over her when they see the smoke of her burning,*
*standing at a distance because of the fear of her torment, saying, 'Woe, woe, the great city, Babylon, the strong city!  For in one hour your judgment has come.'"* Revelation 18:9-10

The prophet Isaiah also saw the destruction of Babylon and the Day of the Lord:
*"Wail, for the Day of the Lord is near!  It will come as destruction from the Almighty.  Therefore all hands will fall limp, and every man's heart will melt.  They will be terrified, pains and anguish will take hold of them; they will writhe like a woman in labor, they will look at one another in astonishment, their faces*

*aflame. Behold, the Day of the Lord is coming, cruel, with fury
and burning anger, to make the land a desolation; and He will
exterminate its sinners from it.*

*For the stars of heaven and their constellations will not
flash forth their light; the sun will be dark when it rises and the
moon will not shed its light.*

*Thus I will punish the world for its evil and the wicked for
their iniquity; I will also put an end to the arrogance of the proud
and abase the haughtiness of the ruthless.*

*I will make mortal man scarcer than pure gold and
Mankind than the gold of Ophir.*

*Therefore I will make the heavens tremble and the earth
will be shaken from its place at the fury of the Lord of hosts in the
day of His burning anger."* <u>Isaiah 13:6-13</u>

While this chapter of Isaiah (Chapter 13) foretold the
fall of the Kingdom of Babylon which would rise after Isaiah's
death, and be destroyed by the Medes some 150 years later,
the above section looks toward the final destruction of
Babylon and tells us of God's plan to rid the world of sinners
as the Millennial Kingdom is set up.

After Babylon is destroyed, Jesus will go to Jerusalem
and destroy the part of the Anti-Christ's army that is fighting
there.

*"In that day His feet will stand on the Mount of Olives,
which is in front of Jerusalem on the east; and the Mount of Olives
will be split in its middle from the east to west by a very large
valley, so the half of the mountain will move to the north and the
other half toward the south"* <u>Zechariah 14:4</u>

*"Now this will be the plague with which the Lord will
strike all the peoples who have gone to war against Jerusalem;
their flesh will rot while they stand on their feet, and their eyes
will rot in the sockets, and their tongue will rot in their mouth."*
<u>Zechariah 14:12</u>

*"For the wine press was trodden outside the city, and blood came out from the wine press, up to the horses' bridles, for a distance of two hundred miles."* Revelation 14:20

He will then move into the valley of Meggido, also known as Jezreel, where the Anti-Christ and his remaining armies are preparing to fight Him:

*"And they gathered them together to the place which in Hebrew is called Armageddon."* Revelation 16:16

*"And I saw the beast and kings of the earth and their armies assembled to make war against Him who sat on the horse and against His army.*
*And the rest were killed with the sword which came from the mouth of Him who sat on the horse, and all the birds were filled with their flesh."* Revelation 19:19, 21

There the Anti-Christ and the False Prophet will be seized and thrown into the lake of fire:

*"And I saw the beast and the kings of the earth and their armies assembled to make war against Him who sat on the horse and against His army.*
*And the beast was seized, and with him the false prophet who performed the signs in his presence, by which he deceived those who had received the mark of the beast and those who worshiped his image; these two were thrown alive into the lake of the fire which burns with brimstone."* Revelation19:19-20

The rest of their armies will be destroyed by *"the sword which came from the mouth of Him who sat on the horse."* Revelation. 19:21

This is probably the same battle described by Joel regarding the destruction of the rest of the armies of the world in the valley of Jehoshaphat.

*"For behold, in those days and at that time, when I restore the fortunes of Judah and Jerusalem,*

*I will gather all the nations and bring them down to the valley of Jehoshaphat. Then I will enter into judgment with them there on behalf of My people and My inheritance, Israel, whom they have scattered among the nations; and they have divided up My land."* Joel 3:1-2

There is currently no valley known as Jehoshaphat, so the location of Joel's description is unknown.

*"Proclaim this among the nations: prepare a war; rouse the mighty men! Let all the soldiers draw near, let them come up!*

*Beat your plowshares into swords and your pruning hooks into spears; let the weak say, "I am a mighty man."*

*Hasten and come, all you surrounding nations, and gather yourselves there. Bring down, O Lord, Your mighty ones.*

*Let the nations be aroused and come up to the valley of Jehoshaphat, for there I will sit to judge all the surrounding nations.*

*Put in the sickle, for harvest is ripe. Come, tread, for the wine press is full; the vats overflow, for their wickedness is great.*

*Multitudes, multitudes in the valley of decision! For the Day of the Lord is near in the valley of decision.*

*The sun and moon grow dark and the stars lose their brightness."* Joel 3:9-15

The Lord will also go into Edom, the area of wilderness southeast of the Dead Sea.

*"Who is this who comes from Edom, with garments of glowing colors from Bozrah? This One who is majestic in His apparel, marching in the greatness of His strength?*

*'It is I who speak in righteousness, mighty to save.' Why is Your apparel red, and Your garments like the one who treads in the wine press?*

*'I have trodden the wine trough alone, and from the peoples there was no man with Me. I also trod them in My anger and trampled them in My wrath; And their lifeblood is sprinkled on My garments, and I stained all My raiment.*

*For the Day of Vengeance was in My Heart, and My year of redemption has come.'"* Isaiah 63:1-4

This may be the location of the "Valley of Jehoshaphat" described by Joel, since King Jehoshaphat did go into Edom and defeated the inhabitants there. (See 2 Kings 3:1-27).

Edom may be where the Jewish believers are being hidden. *"But the two wings of the great eagle were given to the woman* (Israel), *so that she could fly into the wilderness to her place, where she was nourished for a time and times and half a time, from the presence of the serpent."* Revelation 12:14

From Edom, Jesus will go into Egypt and rescue that nation. *"It will become a sign and a witness to the Lord of hosts in the land of Egypt; for they will cry to the Lord because of oppressors, and He will send them a Savior and a Champion, and He will deliver them. Thus the Lord will make Himself known to Egypt, and the Egyptians will know the Lord in that day. They will even worship with sacrifice and offering, and will make a vow to the Lord and perform it."* Isaiah 19:20-21

After all these armies are destroyed, *"all mankind will come to bow down before Me, says the Lord. Then they will go forth and look on the corpses of the men who have transgressed against Me. For their worm will not die and their fire will not be quenched; and they will be an abhorrence to all mankind."* Isaiah 66:23-24

Jesus will then sit on His throne and judge the nations.

*"But when the Son of Man comes in His glory, and all the angels with Him, then he will sit on His glorious throne. All the nations will be gathered before Him; and He will separate them from one another, as the shepherd separates the sheep from the goats; and he will put the sheep on His right, and the goats on the left."* Matthew 25:31-33

This Judgment will be of the living people still left on earth at the end of the Tribulation. All those people who have followed after Him such as the 144,000 saints mentioned above will be placed on His right as His "sheep". Those who are still living at the end of the Tribulation who have opposed Him and His "sheep" will be placed on His left as the "goats". The "goats" will then be cast into Hell with the Anti-Christ and the Prophet.[66]  As noted in Matthew Chapter 25, those people who show mercy and compassion for the brethren or brothers of Jesus, will be judged as "sheep". Those who do not show any mercy or compassion for His brothers will be judged as "goats". Questions have arisen as to whom Jesus meant when he talked about His "brothers". One obvious answer would be all of the Jews and especially the 144,000 preachers. Would it be that anyone who proclaimed Jesus, whether Jew or Gentile, might also be called His brother? This would follow along the teaching of the Good Samaritan parable. Would anyone who shows mercy or compassion for any follower of Jesus during the Tribulation then be judged a "sheep"? This scripture in Matthew seems to say just that. Those who have some mercy and compassion in their hearts will be judged to be righteous

---

[66] The Bible, God through multiple authors; "Then the King will say to those on His right, 'Come, you who are blessed of My Father, inherit the kingdom prepared for you from the foundation of the world. For I was hungry, and you gave Me something to eat; I was thirsty, and you gave Me something to drink; I was a stranger, and you invited Me in; naked, and you clothed Me; I was sick, and you visited Me; I was in prison, and you came to Me.' Then the righteous will answer Him, 'Lord, when did we see You hungry, and feed You, or thirsty, and give You something to drink? And when did we see You a stranger, and invite You in, or naked, and clothe You? When did we see You sick, or in prison, and come to You?' The King will answer and say to them, 'Truly I say to you, to the extent that you did it to one of these brothers of Mine, even the least of them, you did it to Me.' Then He will also say to those on His left, 'Depart from Me, accursed ones, into the eternal fire which has been prepared for the devil and his angels; for I was hungry, and you gave Me nothing to eat; I was thirsty, and you gave Me nothing to drink; I was a stranger, and you did not invite Me in; naked, and you did not clothe Me; sick, and in prison, and you did not visit Me.' Then they themselves also will answer, "Lord, when did we see You hungry, or thirsty, or a stranger, or naked, or sick, or in prison, and did not take care of You?' Then He will answer them, "Truly I say to you, to the extent that you did not do it to one of the least of these, you did not do it to Me.' These will go away into eternal punishment, but the righteous into eternal life." Matthew 25:34-46

"sheep", and will move into the Millennial Kingdom with the Lord.

# CHAPTER 13

# The Millennial
# Kingdom

The Millennial Kingdom is defined by the one thousand year period:

> *"He seized the dragon, that ancient serpent, who is the devil, or Satan, and bound him for a thousand years. He threw him into the Abyss, and locked and sealed it over him, to keep him from deceiving the nations anymore until the thousand years were ended. After that, he must be set free for a short time.*
>
> *I saw thrones on which were seated those who had been given authority to judge. And I saw the souls of those who had been beheaded because of their testimony about Jesus and because of the word of God.*
>
> *They had not worshiped the beast or its image and had not received its mark on their foreheads or their hands. They came to life and reigned with Christ a thousand years. (The rest of the dead did not come to life until the thousand years were ended.)*
>
> *This is the first resurrection. Blessed and holy are those who share in the first resurrection. The second death has no*

*power over them, but they will be priests of God and of Christ and will reign with him for a thousand years."* <u>Revelation 20:2-6</u>

Satan is bound throughout this thousand year time, and life on earth approaches the original design.

Daniel saw this kingdom and described it to the King Nebuchadnezzar:

*"In the time of those kings, the God of heaven will set up a kingdom that will never be destroyed, nor will it be left to another people. It will crush all those kingdoms and bring them to an end, but it will itself endure forever."* <u>Daniel 2:44</u>

Daniel was explaining the dream that the King had concerning a large statue made of different metals. The feet were made of iron, while its ten toes were made of iron and clay mixed together describing the ten kings and their "kingdoms" forming the World Government. Daniel continued to explain the dream to the king:

*"You continued looking until a stone was cut out without hands, and it struck the statue on its feet of iron and clay and crushed them.*
*Then the iron, the clay, the bronze, the silver, and the gold were crushed all at the same time and became like chaff from the summer threshing floors; and the wind carried them away so that not a trace of them was found. But the stone that struck the statue became a great mountain and filled the whole earth."* <u>Daniel 2:34-35</u>

Daniel here revealed that God would destroy the revived Roman Empire (One-World Kingdom) and replace it with His own Millennial Kingdom that would encompass the entire earth.

The major and overarching reality of the Millennial Kingdom is that Jesus will be King of Kings and Lord of Lords over the entire world (<u>Revelation 11:15</u>).

*"And the Lord will be King over all the earth; in that day the Lord will be the only one, and His name the only one."* Zechariah 14:9

The words of Isaiah will be fulfilled:

*"For a child will be born to us, a son will be given to us; and the government will rest on His shoulders; and His name will be called Wonderful Counselor, Mighty God, Eternal Father, Prince of Peace.*

*There will be no end to the increase of His government or of peace, on the throne of David and over his kingdom, to establish it and to uphold it with justice and righteousness from then on and forevermore."* Isaiah 9:6-7

*"Thus says the Lord, 'I will return to Zion and will dwell in the midst of Jerusalem."* Zechariah 8:3

*"So many peoples and mighty nations will come to seek the Lord of hosts in Jerusalem and to entreat the favor of the Lord."* Zechariah 8:22

In that day, everyone in the world will acknowledge that Jesus is Lord over all.

*"...so that at the name of Jesus every knee will bow, of those who are in heaven and on earth and under the earth,*

*and that every tongue will confess that Jesus Christ is Lord, to the glory of God the Father."* Philippians 2:10-11

*"And behold, with the clouds of heaven One like a Son of Man was coming, and he came up to the Ancient of Days and was presented before Him.*

*And to him was given dominion, glory and a kingdom, that all the peoples, nations and men of every language might serve Him. His dominion is an everlasting dominion which will not pass away; and His kingdom is one which will not be destroyed."* Daniel 7:13-14

Not all will accept Jesus as Lord willingly.

*"Then it will come about that any who are left of all the nations that went against Jerusalem will go up from year to year to worship the King, the Lord of hosts, and to celebrate the Feast of Booths.*

*And it will be that whichever of the families of the earth does not go up to Jerusalem to worship the King, the Lord of hosts, there will be no rain on them."* Zechariah 14:16-17

These verses of Zechariah inform us that there will be people alive at the end of the Tribulation who have not accepted Jesus as Lord, but have the capacity of mercy and compassion.  Everyone will recognize that Jesus is Lord of the world, but not everyone will embrace Him.  Also, people will be born during the Millennium who will continue to manifest Original Sin, and rebel against God in some form.  This rebellion will come to a head at the end of the thousand years.

The topology of Israel will be greatly changed, possibly during the Great Earthquake of the seventh Bowl of Wrath.  Jerusalem will be elevated on a type of mesa, and the mountains around it will be lowered and the area south of Jerusalem reduced to a plain.

*"All the land will be changed into a plain from Geba to Rimmon south of Jerusalem; but Jerusalem will rise and remain on its site from Benjamin's Gate as far as the place of the First Gate to the Corner Gate, and from the tower of Hananel to the king's wine presses."* Zechariah 14:10

*"Now it will come about that in the last days the mountain of the house of the Lord will be established as the chief of the mountains, and will be raised above the hills..."* Isaiah 2:2

*"And it will come about in the last days that the mountain of the house of the Lord will be established as the chief of the mountains, it will be raised above the hills..."* Micah 4:1

A river will run out of Jerusalem, both to the east running into the Dead Sea, and to the west, running into the Mediterranean Sea. The river will begin on the Temple Mount and actually come out of the Millennial temple.

*"And in that day living waters will flow out of Jerusalem, half of them toward the eastern sea and the other half toward the western sea..."* Zechariah 14:8

*"...And a spring will go out from the house of the Lord to water the valley of Shittim."* Joel 3:18

*"Then he brought me back to the door of the house; and behold, water was flowing from under the threshold of the house toward the east*

*...then he said to me, These waters go out toward the eastern region and go down into the Arabah; then they go toward the sea, being made to flow into the sea, and the waters of the sea become fresh."* Ezekiel 47:1, 8

The river flowing from the temple into the Dead Sea will probably run through the new valley opened up when Jesus stands on the Mount of Olives. At that time, the mountain will split in two parts, one part moving north, and one part moving south, forming a new valley running toward the Dead Sea. The Dead Sea's salinity level is so high that no fish have ever been found there. However, when this miraculous river runs into it, it will become a living sea with fish and wildlife.

*"It will come about that every living creature which swarms in every place where the river goes, will live. And there will be very many fish, for these waters go there and the others become fresh; so everything will live where the river goes.*

*And it will come about that fishermen will stand beside it; from Engedi to Eneglaim there will be a place for the spreading of nets. Their fish will be according to their kinds, like the fish of the Great Sea, very many.*

203

*But its swamps and marshes will not become fresh; they will be left for salt."* Ezekiel 47:9-11

So Jerusalem will be elevated with all the lands south of it forming a plain, and rivers flowing out of Jerusalem to the east and west.

The promise of plentiful waters will be fulfilled at this time.

*"...And I will cause showers to come down in their season; they will be showers of blessing. Also the tree of the field will yield its fruit and the earth will yield its increase, and they will be secure on their land."* Ezekiel 34:26-27

*"...This desolate place has become like the garden of Eden..."* Ezekiel 36:35

*"I will open rivers on the bare heights and springs in the midst of the valleys; I will make the wilderness a pool of water and the dry land fountains of water.*
*I will put the cedar in the wilderness, the acacia and the myrtle and the olive tree; I will place the juniper in the desert together with the box tree and the cypress."* Isaiah 41:18-19

This will be a time of wondrous happenings. Immortal saints will rule the world under King Jesus, and mortal men will live long peaceful lives.

*"Then I saw thrones, and they sat on them, and judgment was given to them. And I saw the souls of those who had been beheaded because of their testimony of Jesus and because of the word of God, and those who had not worshiped the beast or his image, and had not received the mark on the forehead and on their hand; and they came to life and reigned with Christ for a thousand years."* Revelation 20:4

*"He who overcomes, and he who keeps My deeds until the end, to him I will give authority over the nations; and he shall rule*

*them with a rod of iron, as the vessels of the potter are broken to pieces, as I also have received authority from My Father..."* Revelation2:26-27

*"He who overcomes, I will grant to him to sit down with Me on My throne, as I also overcame and sat down with My Father on His throne."* Revelation 3:21

*"...Do you not know that the saints will judge the world?"* 1 Corinthians 6:2

*"Then the sovereignty, power and greatness of all the kingdoms under heaven will be handed over to the holy people of the Most High. His kingdom will be an everlasting kingdom, and all rulers will worship and obey him."* Daniel 7:27

The immortal saints of the Church Age and the Tribulation will be the rulers of the world under the authority of Jesus.

Mortal men who come through the Tribulation or are born during that era will once again live very long lives. They will be restored to the physical state of the people born before the Great Flood.

*"Never again will there be in it an infant who lives but a few days, or an old man who does not live out his years; the one who dies at a hundred will be thought a mere child; the one who fails to reach a hundred will be considered accursed..*
*They will build houses and dwell in them; they will plant vineyards and eat their fruit. No longer will they build houses and others live in them, or plant and others eat.*
*For as the days of a tree, so will be the days of my people; my chosen ones will long enjoy the work of their hands."* Isaiah 65:20-22

This will be a kingdom that restores and fulfills the covenant of God for the Jews.

*"He will raise a banner for the nations and gather the exiles of Israel; he will assemble the scattered people of Judah from the four quarters of the earth*

*...The LORD will dry up the gulf of the Egyptian sea; with a scorching wind he will sweep his hand over the Euphrates River. He will break it up into seven streams so that anyone can cross over in sandals..*

*There will be a highway for the remnant of his people that is left from Assyria, as there was for Israel when they came up from Egypt."* Isaiah 11:12,15-16

Jews from all over the world will come to Israel, where they will be honored as the People of God.

*"As a shepherd looks after his scattered flock when he is with them, so will I look after my sheep. I will rescue them from all the places where they were scattered on a day of clouds and darkness.*

*I will bring them out from the nations and gather them from the countries, and I will bring them into their own land.*

*I will pasture them on the mountains of Israel, in the ravines and in all the settlements in the land."* Ezekiel 34:12-13

God is restoring the Kingdom of Israel for His Own sake, not for the sake of His people. He is fulfilling His promises to Abraham, Isaac, Jacob and David.

*"Therefore say to the Israelites, 'This is what the Sovereign LORD says: It is not for your sake, people of Israel, that I am going to do these things, but for the sake of my holy name, which you have profaned among the nations where you have gone. I will show the holiness of my great name, which has been profaned among the nations, the name you have profaned among them.*

*Then the nations will know that I am the LORD, declares the Sovereign LORD, when I am proved holy through you before their eyes. 'For I will take you out of the nations; I will gather you from all the countries and bring you back into your own land. I will sprinkle clean water on you, and you will be clean; I will cleanse you from all your impurities and from all your idols.*

*I will give you a new heart and put a new spirit in you; I will remove from you your heart of stone and give you a heart of flesh. And I will put my Spirit in you and move you to follow my decrees and be careful to keep my laws. Then you will live in the land I gave your ancestors; you will be my people, and I will be your God."* Ezekiel 36:22-28

Not only will the Jews live in their own land, but God will put His new covenant into them, and pour out the Holy Spirit on them.

*They will live in the land I gave to my servant Jacob, the land where your ancestors lived. They and their children and their children's children will live there forever,*
*and David my servant will be their prince forever. I will make a covenant of peace with them; it will be an everlasting covenant. I will establish them and increase their numbers, and I will put my sanctuary among them forever.*
*My dwelling place will be with them; I will be their God, and they will be my people. Then the nations will know that I the LORD make Israel holy, when my sanctuary is among them forever.'"* Ezekiel 37:25-28

Jesus will sit on the throne of David over the entire world, and perhaps the resurrected David will be King again over Israel!

As noted above, the Millennial Kingdom will have a Temple, which will be built by Jesus Himself.

*"...Here is the man whose name is the Branch, and he will branch out from his place and build the temple of the LORD. **It is he who will build the temple of the LORD,***
*and he will be clothed with majesty and will sit and rule*

*on his throne. And he will be a priest on his throne. And there will be harmony between the two."* <u>Zechariah 6:12-13</u>

This is a wonderful vision of our Lord Jesus when He comes and fulfills both roles as Ruler of the earth and Priest for His people. The Jews have a concept of two messiahs, one the son of Joseph and the other the son of David. The son of Joseph will redeem and save the Jews as Joseph did when his family came down into Egypt during the great famine. The son of David will rule over the Jews as David did. Jesus has come in one of the roles already, the Redeemer and Savior. When He returns He will fulfill the other role as Ruler of the earth.

Ezekiel (Chapters 40-44) describes the temple as shown him in a vision. (The third Tribulation Temple will be totally or partially destroyed during the Anti-Christ's attack on Jerusalem. The purpose of this fourth temple, usually referred to as the Millennial Temple, is not totally clear at this time. There is much speculation about finding the Ark of the Covenant again. Archeological digs under the Temple Mount have come close to an area described by the Jewish Archeologists as full of the Presence of God. Yet these digs were closed at the insistence of the Muslims, who claimed (and still do to this day) that the Mount belongs to them. God revealed the actual future regarding the Ark to Jeremiah, as follows:

*"Then I will give you shepherds after my own heart, who will lead you with knowledge and understanding.*

*In those days, when your numbers have increased greatly in the land," declares the LORD, "people will no longer say, 'The ark of the covenant of the LORD.'*

*It will never enter their minds or be remembered; it will not be missed, nor will another one be made.*

*At that time they will call Jerusalem The Throne of the LORD, and all nations will gather in Jerusalem to honor the name of the LORD.*

*No longer will they follow the stubbornness of their evil hearts." Jeremiah 3:15-17*

These verses indicate that the Ark of the Covenant will not be found again, or if it is, will be destroyed (or declared "secondary" in the presence of Jesus Himself) before the Millennium.

Some Jewish Christians such as Zola Levitt[67] have reminded us that the Church will be taken off of the earth either before or during the Tribulation by the Rapture. After that, the only people on earth who know about God will be the Jews. However, Tim LaHaye and Jerry Jenkins, in their <u>Left Behind</u> series imagine an underground Christian Church during the Tribulation that continues to bring people to Jesus.[68] Certainly, all men will bow down to Jesus as King of Kings, and the writer of Hebrews reminds us that His sacrifice on the cross removed forever the need to offer more sacrifices to God.[69]

Some have asked why God would want a Millennial Kingdom. We certainly do not know all of God's intentions for His creation, and we cannot clearly fathom the true purpose of the Millennium from what has been revealed.

---

[67] <u>The Seven Feasts of Israel</u>, Zola Levitt, 1979; Zola Levitt Ministries, Dallas, Texas

[68] <u>Left Behind (Series)</u>, Tim LaHaye and Jerry Jenkins, 1995-2004, Tyndale House Publishers

[69] <u>The Bible</u>, God through many authors, *"And by that will, we have been made holy through the sacrifice of the body of Jesus Christ once for all. Day after day every priest stands and performs his religious duties; again and again he offers the same sacrifices, which can never take away sins. But when this priest had offered for all time one sacrifice for sins, he sat down at the right hand of God, and since that time he waits for his enemies to be made his footstool. For by one sacrifice he has made perfect forever those who are being made holy."*<u>Hebrews 10:10-14</u>

However, some have speculated that it will be a time of memorial for all of the old Jewish saints who lived before the coming of Jesus. Another explanation may be that it will be a time of transition for the Jews and all of remaining mankind, and certainly a time of God's fulfillment of His covenants with the Patriarchs, and His promises through the Prophets.

There is an ancient prophecy about the time span for the world. Both Jewish rabbis and post-apostolic Church fathers wrote about the 7000 year prophecy: Two thousand years from Adam to Abraham, two thousand years from Abraham to Messiah (Jesus), two thousand years of the Gentiles (Church Age), and a thousand year "Sabbath" for the world. The Millennium is the 1000 year time of rest before the final destruction of the physical world.

But whatever, God's reason, as noted in Ezekiel 36:22-28, God will be the Shepherd for the Jews, and demonstrate His love for them to the entire world. The Jews will be elevated in status among men because of God's love and favor for them.

*"This is what the LORD Almighty says: "I am very jealous for Zion; I am burning with jealousy for her...*
*I will return to Zion and dwell in Jerusalem.*
*Then Jerusalem will be called the Faithful City, and the mountain of the LORD Almighty will be called the Holy Mountain."* Zechariah 8:2-3

God wants the entire world to know where His heart is centered and where He can be found during the Millennium.

*"This is what the LORD Almighty says: "Many peoples and the inhabitants of many cities will yet come, and the inhabitants of one city will go to another and say, 'Let us go at once to entreat the LORD and seek the LORD Almighty. I myself am going.'*

*And many peoples and powerful nations will come to Jerusalem to seek the LORD Almighty and to entreat him.*

*This is what the LORD Almighty says: "In those days ten people from all languages and nations will take firm hold of one Jew by the hem of his robe and say, 'Let us go with you, because we have heard that God is with you.'"* Zechariah 8:20-23

God will honor the Jews, and people of the world will seek them out to honor them.

The Millennium will be a time of world-wide peace, not only among men, but also in nature. This is the "Peaceable Kingdom" of art and stories of old.

*"...They will beat their swords into plowshares and their spears into pruning hooks. Nation will not take up sword against nation, nor will they train for war anymore."* Micah 4:3

With Satan bound and out of the world, people will not wage wars again—at least, not until he is released at the end of the thousand years.

*"The wolf and the lamb will feed together, and the lion will eat straw like the ox, and dust will be the serpent's food. They will neither harm nor destroy on all my holy mountain,..."* Isaiah 65:25

*"The wolf will live with the lamb, the leopard will lie down with the goat, the calf and the lion and the yearling together; and a little child will lead them, The cow will feed with the bear, their young will lie down together, and the lion will eat straw like the ox.*

*The infant will play near the cobra's den, and the young child will put its hand into the viper's nest.*

*They will neither harm nor destroy on all my holy mountain, for the earth will be filled with the knowledge of the LORD as the waters cover the sea."* Isaiah 11:6-9

211

The world will be in balance again. Men will not fear other men, and everyone will know the Lord and His ordinances. The Saints will settle disputes with truth and justice. All peoples will live in peace, and will not have to worry about their health or wealth. Crops will be abundant and families will be strong.

# CHAPTER 14

# The Final Rebellion

# &

# The White Throne

# Judgment

At the end of the Millennium, a world-wide revolt will occur.

*"When the thousand years are over, Satan will be released from his prison,*
*and will go out to deceive the nations in the four corners of the earth--Gog and Magog--to gather them for battle. In number they are like the sand on the seashore.*
*They marched across the breadth of the earth and surrounded the camp of God's people, the city He loves. But fire came down from heaven and devoured them.*
*And the devil who deceived them was thrown into the lake of burning sulfur, where the beast and the false prophet had been*

*thrown. They will be tormented day and night for ever and ever."* Revelation 20:7-10

Could it be that during the Millennium, mankind's hearts become hard and proud again? Obviously, there will be a huge number of mortals who are easily deceived by Satan and join the rebellion as noted in the verses above. It is during and after this rebellion that the surface of the earth will be destroyed.

*"But the day of the Lord will come like a thief. The heavens will disappear with a roar; the elements will be destroyed by fire, and the earth and everything in it will be laid bare."* 2 Peter 3:10

*"Behold, the Lord lays the earth waste, devastates it, distorts its surface and scatters its inhabitants...the earth will be completely laid waste and completely despoiled, for the Lord has spoken this word."* Isaiah 24:1, 3

*"'I will sweep away everything from the face of the earth,"* declares the Lord. *'I will sweep away both men and animals; I will sweep away the birds of the air and the fish of the sea.'"* Zephaniah 1:2-3

*"And all the earth will be devoured in the fire of His jealousy, for He will make a complete end, indeed a terrifying one, of all the inhabitants of the earth."* Zephaniah1:18

And so the first earth and heavens will pass away, to give room for the eternal New Earth and Heavens.

At the end of the Millennium and the Final Rebellion, Jesus will judge all people at the Great White Throne.

*"Then I saw a great white throne and Him who was seated on it. Earth and sky fled from His presence, and there was no place for them.*
*And I saw the dead, great and small, standing before the*

*throne, and books were opened. Another book was opened, which is the book of life. The dead were judged according to what they had done as recorded in the books.*

*The sea gave up the dead that were in it, and death and Hades gave up the dead that were in them, and each person was judged according to what they had done.*

*Then death and Hades were thrown into the lake of fire. The lake of fire is the second death.*

*If anyone's name was not found written in the book of life, he was thrown into the lake of fire."* Revelation 20:11-15

All of the dead who were not involved in the first resurrection will be judged at this time, including the fallen angels who have followed Satan. Men and women will be judged by their actions, but without the covering of the blood of Jesus. All those who have accepted the Lordship of Jesus, and thus their sins have been covered by His blood, will not be a part of this terrible judgment. This will be the final judgment, and death will be no more.

# CHAPTER 15

# The New Earth and Heavens

Once the old Earth goes through the refining fires over the surface, the New Earth and Heavens are revealed. This is the resurrection of the Creation that Paul mentions in <u>Romans 8:19-23</u>.

*"For the creation waits with eager expectation for the children of God to be revealed.*

*For the creation was subjected to frustration, not by its own choice but by the will of him who subjected it, in hope that the creation itself will be liberated from its bondage to decay and brought into the freedom and glory of the children of God.*

*We know that the whole creation has been groaning as in the pains of childbirth right up to the present time. Not only so, but we ourselves, who have the first fruits of the spirit, groan inwardly as we wait eagerly for our adoption to sonship, the redemption of our bodies."*

After the refining of the surface of the earth, the New Earth, the eternal state is brought forth from God.

*"See, I will create new heavens and a new earth. The former things will not be remembered nor will they come to mind."* Isaiah 65:17

John saw the same vision as he reported in Revelations 21:1-4,

*"Then I saw a new heaven and a new earth; for the first heaven and the first earth had passed away, and there was no longer any sea.*

*And I saw the Holy City, the new Jerusalem, coming down out of heaven from God, prepared as a bride beautifully dressed for her husband.*

*And I heard a loud voice from the throne saying, 'Look! God's dwelling place is now among the people, and He will dwell with them. They will be his people, and God himself will be with them and be their God.*

*He will wipe away every tear from their eyes. There will be no more death or mourning or crying or pain, for the old order of things has passed away.'"*

C. S. Lewis described the New Narnia in the last of his Narnia Chronicles, The Last Battle. The main characters of the stories have found themselves in a new land that is similar but different from the Narnia they had known previously. Lord Digory finally sees what the difference is. "Listen, Peter. When Aslan said you could never go back to Narnia, he meant the Narnia you were thinking of. But that was not the real Narnia. That had a beginning and an end. It was only a shadow or a copy of the real Narnia which has always been here and always will be here: just as our own world is only a shadow or copy of something in Aslan's real world. ...Of course it is different; as different as a real thing is from a shadow or as waking life is from a dream."[70] So the New Earth will be much more wonderful than we can imagine. We will have new immortal bodies that will be able to do incredible things, again much more than we can imagine.

---

[70] The Last Battle, C.S. Lewis, HarperTrophy, 1956, pp. 194-195

God will live on Earth with us. Randy Alcorn states, "The New Earth will be the setting for God's Kingdom. The New Jerusalem will be where people come to pay Him tribute."[71] Alcorn then quotes Isaiah 66:22-23:

"'As the new heavens and the new earth that I make will endure before me,' declares the Lord, 'so will your name and descendants endure...All mankind will come and bow down before me,' says the Lord."

The curse placed on the old (current) earth at the time of the Fall of Man (Genesis 3:15-19) will be lifted at the time of the Resurrection of Creation. Revelation 22:3 states, "There will no longer be any curse..." indicating that the old hardships brought into creation at the time of the Fall will no longer be present. The Curse was on the earth and the man and woman.

"And I will put enmity
between you and the woman,
and between your seed and her seed;
He shall bruise you on the head,
and you shall bruise him on the heel.

To the woman He said,
'I will greatly multiply your pain in childbirth,
in pain you will bring forth children;
yet your desire will be for your husband,
and he will rule over you.'

Then to Adam He said, 'Because you have listened to the voice of your wife, and have eaten from the tree about which I commanded you, saying, 'You shall not eat from it': Cursed is the ground because of you; in toil you will eat of it all the days of your life.

Both thorns and thistles it shall grow for you; and you will eat the plants of the field;

---

[71] Heaven, Randy Alcorn, Tyndale House Publishers, 2004; p. 148

*by the sweat of your face*
*you will eat bread...'"* <u>Genesis 3:15-19</u>

Imagine growing vegetables and flowers without having to deal with fertilizer or weeds. Plants will not need to be cultivated, providing fruits, vegetables, and flowers almost at will. While many have postulated that there will be no mountains, I think that God has in store for us a world of much greater physical beauty than anything we have ever seen. We will indeed be in Heaven, a place of no tears and no bad memories. I can hardly wait.

# CHAPTER 16

# Epilogue

We have reviewed a few of the prophecies that God has given us through the writers of the Bible to help us understand the events surrounding us as we move toward the End Times. His promises for our futures and the world's future remind how wonderful our Lord is. Others worry and fret about the future of the world, but we actually have the plans in our hands. We know what the future holds.

The thesis of this book is to remind us that we can anticipate the "End Times". When Jesus gave us the parable of the Fig Leaves, and the proverb of the vultures he was showing us that when we see one sign, we shouldn't be too concerned. But when two signs or better yet, multiple signs start showing up, we should really get ready for the return of our Lord.

Christian TV shows have guests talking about the End Times frequently. I think more Christians are "feeling" the time is getting closer. Obviously this book is designed to help us see and understand the signs.

In summary, the signs, or Fig Leaves are as follows:

1. Nation vs. nation; kingdom vs. kingdom
2. Plagues
3. Earthquakes
4. Famines
5. Hatred of Christians
6. Apostasy
7. Deception
8. Lawlessness
9. Loss of Love
10. Gospel Preached in the whole world
11. Abomination of Desolation
12. Great Tribulation
13. Great Signs in the Heavens
14. The Sign in the Sky before The Second Coming of Jesus (Yeshua)
15. Restoration of Israel
16. Blossoming of the land of Israel
17. Prosperity of Israel
18. Security of Israel
19. Failed Russo-Iranian Invasion of Israel (Magog/Persia)
20. Redemption of Egypt and Iraq by the Lord
21. Highway Running between Egypt and Iraq through Israel
22. (Rise of the Anti-Christ)
23. (One World Government)
24. (God's Trumpet Judgments)
25. (God's Bowl Judgments)

By the time the Anti-Christ arises, and the tribulation begins along with the One World Government and God's judgments are poured out, most people familiar with God's word will know what is happening. Currently, Fig Leaves #1-8 as related by Jesus are being revealed more every day. Number 10 (Gospel preached throughout the world) is approaching completion. The restoration of Israel (#15) has begun and is continuing to "grow." The signs of prosperity, blossoming and security of Israel (#16-18) are in various stages of completion. The "early" signs are showing already. When the story breaks that Russia and Iran have come together to "solve" the Israel "problem", you will know that another of God's great signs is about to occur (#19).

Remember the words of Paul and Peter:

*"But mark this: There will be terrible times in the last days. People will be lovers of themselves, lovers of money, boastful, proud, abusive, disobedient to their parents, ungrateful, unholy, without love, unforgiving, slanderous, without self-control, brutal, not lovers of the good, treacherous, rash, conceited, lovers of pleasure rather than lovers of God— having a form of godliness but denying its power. Have nothing to do with such people."* 2 Timothy 3:1-5

*"Above all, you must understand that in the last days scoffers will come, scoffing and following their own evil desires. They will say, "Where is this 'coming' he promised? Ever since our ancestors died, everything goes on as it has since the beginning of creation."*
*But they deliberately forget that long ago by God's word the heavens came into being and the earth was formed out of water and by water. By these waters also the world of that time was deluged and destroyed.*
*By the same word the present heavens and earth are reserved for fire, being kept for the day of judgment and destruction of the ungodly.*
*But do not forget this one thing, dear friends: With the Lord a day is like a thousand years, and a thousand years are like a day. The Lord is not slow in keeping his promise, as some understand slowness. Instead he is patient with you, not wanting anyone to perish, but everyone to come to repentance."* 2 Peter 3:3-9

Certainly we are seeing more "mockers" of the faith. And we are seeing more people succumbing to secularism and other idols. This certainly feels like the times described by Paul and Peter.

The purpose of prophecy is to edify the Church. The Fig Leaves discussed here are not something that gives us "special" knowledge so that we know something that others do not know. For those of us in His Church, as we see more of God's prophecies revealed in the current events of the day, we should get more serious about telling everyone we know about the Gospel. We do not want to have Jesus call us lukewarm when we stand before Him. As the world grows darker and colder, His Church should be brighter and warmer, attracting people to Him.

The members of His Church are God's feet and hands, and we are moving into a period of time where our actions are becoming more important. It is a time to be on fire for Jesus. It is a time to let everyone know God's plan of salvation: the sacrifice of His son, Yeshua (Jesus in the Greek) so that the Blood of Yeshua covers and redeems all who earnestly seek God. Remember the words of the angel to Daniel:

*"Those who are wise will shine brightly like the brightness of the heavens, and those who lead many to righteousness, like the stars for ever and ever."* Daniel 12:3

We should always remember that we are not fighting against those people who are opposing Christianity. As Paul said, *"...our struggle is not against flesh and blood, but against the powers, against the world forces of this darkness, against the spiritual forces of wickedness in the heavenly places."* Ephesians 6:12

God made all the people of the earth and He loves them all, and wants all to be saved. Peter reminds us that the Lord has delayed His judgment on earth because *"..(He) is patient toward you, not wishing for any to perish but for all to come to repentance."* 2 Peter 3:9.

We should be beacons of God's love for those who may be mocking and abusing Him and us. They are walking in great darkness.  We should be light and salt for them in these perilous days.

In speaking about the Blood of Jesus, a verse from Matthew has been used for centuries to imply that all Jews were/are guilty of putting Jesus to death.

*"All the people answered, "His blood be on us and on our children.""* <u>Matthew 27:25</u>

The anti-Semitism that has been released through the Church because of this passage has been horrendous.[72] Recently, I read a statement from one of my Jewish brothers in Christ who said he hoped that someday soon, the Blood of Yeshua would indeed cover all of God's chosen people, as it does those of us in His Church.  What a wonderful perspective that shows God's ultimate intent for that passage.

As more Fig Leaves are revealed, let us feel the urgency to work for God, for time is indeed short.

The final words in Revelation are:
*Then He told me, "Do not seal up the words of the prophecy of this scroll, for the **time is near.***

*Let the one who is wrong, still do wrong; and the one who is filthy, still be filthy; and let the one who is righteous, still practice righteousness; and the one who is holy, still keep himself holy.*

*Look, I am coming soon! My reward is with Me, and I will give to each person according to what they have done.  I am the Alpha and the Omega, the First and the Last, the Beginning and the End."*

*Blessed are those who wash their robes, that they may have the right to the tree of life, and may go through the gates into the city. Outside are the dogs, those who practice magic arts, the sexually immoral, the murders, the idolaters, and everyone who loves and practices falsehood.*

---

[72] <u>Our Hands Are Stained With Blood</u>, Michael L. Brown; Destiny Image Publishers, Inc., 1992

"I, Jesus, have sent My angel to give you this testimony for the churches. I am the Root and the Offspring of David, the bright Morning Star."

The Spirit and the bride say, "Come!" And let the one who hears say, "Come!" Let the one who is thirsty come; and let the one who wishes take the free gift of the water of life.

I warn everyone who hears the words of the prophecy of this scroll" If anyone adds anything to them, God will add to that person the plagues described in this scroll.

And if anyone takes words away from this scroll of prophecy, God will take away from that person any share in the tree of life and in the Holy City, which are described in this scroll.

He who testifies to these things says, "Yes, I am coming soon." Amen. Come, Lord Jesus.

The grace of the Lord Jesus be with God's people. Amen.
Revelation 22:10-21

And so we, who follow our Lord echo with all we have, "Come, Lord Jesus!"

# For Anyone Reading This Book Who Is Not a Christian

First, thank you if have read up to this point in the book. It must have seemed foolish and insignificant to you. However, I want to say this: There is a God in Heaven! I know that science indicates that there is no place in outer space that could be called "Heaven." From a scientific standpoint, heaven is in another dimension. Cosmologists, those who consider the "Big Picture" of the universe, currently use Superstring Theory to try to explain the origin of and maintenance of this universe. String theory, as it is known, actually postulates 10 dimensions with many alternative universes. So other dimensions are clearly within the concepts of the most brilliant minds on earth. Visits to this world by angels reveal that they can just appear and disappear, while being very tangible while here. (See *Angels on Assignment* by Roland Buck, 1979).

I would ask you to investigate the prophecies cited in this book and understand that the God who created this world (and universe) placed these in the Bible so that humans could understand that there is an extraterrestrial being out there who knows all of the answers. He knows the end story for all of us. Time is one of the dimensions of this universe, and is therefore part of the creation. The dimension of Heaven where God dwells has no such parameter as Time. God actually can see the Future as well as He sees the Past.

I know this sounds strange to the ears of someone inculcated in the ideology of "Natural Causes." But you should understand that all you have been taught regarding "reality" are the ideas and thoughts of other men and women. So no matter how convincing they sound, they are merely someone else's thoughts. Only in the Bible do you find the Truths that come from the One Person who knows not only all of the secrets of the universe, but also knows you.

Please know that you are loved. God loves you, even if you reject that He is real. And because God loves you, you will find that those people who follow him with all of their heart will love you too. But beware of those wolves in sheep's clothing who call themselves Christians but follow their own agendas.

May God bless you as you read His Word, and may you find the peace and joy that you have been seeking.

# Prophetic Bible Verses

Below are some of the verses in the Bible that are prophetic. The verses are generally chronological from each book. While some verses from Revelation are listed, the entire book is prophetic.

| | | |
|---|---|---|
| Isaiah | 2:2-4 | Jerusalem will be raised up; Ezekiel 40:2, Micah 4:1, Zechariah 14:10 No more war |
| | 4:1-6 | Jewish remnant will be holy/ Light all of the time |
| | 9:6-7 | Jesus will reign as King of Kings |
| | 11:1-5 | Jesus will reign as King of Kings |
| | 11:6-9 | Peace over the whole earth |
| | 11:11 | The second restoration of Israel |
| | 11:15 | The Nile will be dried up; c.f. Isaiah 19:5-8 and Revelation 16:8-12 |
| | 11:16 | Highway from Iraq |
| | 13:6-16 | Judgment on Day of the Lord |
| | 18:7 | Ethiopians will bring gifts to Jerusalem |

| 19:3-4 | After the Magog war, Egypt will be under the King of the South and then the Antichrist |
| 19:5-8 | The Nile will dry up |
| 19:16-19 | Egypt will fear Israel & begin to turn to the Lord |
| 19:20 | Jesus will deliver Egypt from the Antichrist (Armageddon) |
| 19:21-25 | Egypt will turn to the Lord and become a blessing |
| 24:1-23 | The Apocalypse of Isaiah (The Destruction of Earth) |
| 32:1-8 | People in the Millennium will have discernment |
| 32:15-18 | The Spirit poured out |
| 33:5-6 | The Lord is Exalted |
| 33:17-24 | The King will reign |
| 35:1-10 | The New Kingdom; No fear; there will be gladness and joy |
| 41:17-20 | The New Kingdom will be bountiful |
| 44:3-4 | Springs of water in the New Kingdom |
| 60:1-22 | Zion Glorified |
| 62:1-12 | Zion's Glory and a new name (v. 2) |
| 65:17-25 | New Earth and Heaven |
| 66:15-16 | The Lord's Vengence |
| 66:17-24 | The New Kingdom |

| | | |
|---|---|---|
| Ezekiel 34:23-29 | God's Covenant for peace and safety |
| 36:25-30 | God's Redemption of His people |
| 36:34-35 | Israel will be like the Garden of Eden |
| 37:24-28 | The Davidic Kingdom |
| 40-46 | The Millennial Temple |
| 40:2 | A very high mountain |
| 47:1-12 | The River flowing from the temple to the East |
| 47:7 | Trees on both sides; c.f. Revelation 22 and Zechariah 14:8 |
| Daniel 2:44-45 | The Divine Kingdom |
| 7:13-14 | The Son of Man and His Eternal Kingdom |
| 7:27 | The Eternal Kingdom of God |
| Micah 4:1 | The Mountain of the Lord will be Raised |
| 4:2-3 | The Nations will come to the Lord for Judgment |
| 4:4-7 | All will be secure and safe |
| Joel 3:18,20 | Judah will be bountiful and inhabited forever |
| Zechariah | |
| 2:10-12 | The Lord will live in Jerusalem again |

| | |
|---|---|
| 6:12-15 | The Branch (Yeshua) will build the temple of the Lord |
| 8:1-23 | The Lord will return to Zion and live in Jerusalem; The Divine Kingdom will be established |
| 13:1-2 | A Fountain for healing and the removal of all idols |
| 14:8 | A river will flow out of Jerusalem to the seas |
| 14:9 | The Lord will reign over all the world |
| 14:10 | Jerusalem will rise above the rest of the country |
| 14:11 | Jerusalem will be safe and secure |
| 14:16-19 | All nations will come to Jerusalem for the Feast of Booths or suffer drought |
| 14:20-21 | Everything in Jerusalem and Judah will be Holy to the Lord |

Revelation

| | |
|---|---|
| 2:26-28 | The Saints will be given authority over the nations |
| 3:5-6 | The Saints will be given white garments and the Lord will confess their names before the Father |
| 3:12 | Yeshua will make the Saints the pillars of the new Temple, and will write the name of God on them, and the name of the new Jerusalem, and His new name |

| | |
|---|---|
| 3:21 | The Saints will sit down with Jesus on His throne |
| 7:15 | The Kingdom of the Lord will reign forever |
| 20:2-4 | Satan bound for a thousand years; the Saints reign with Jesus for a thousand years |

# Bibliography

The Late Great Planet Earth, Hal Lindsey, Zondervan Publishing House, 1970

Vine's Expository Dictionary of Old and New Testament Words, ed. F.F. Bruce, Fleming H. Revell Co., 1981

Dictionary of Theological Terms, Alan Cairns, Ambassador-Emerald International, 2002.

Every Prophecy of the Bible, John F. Walvoord, David C. Cook, 1999

The Antiquities of the Jews, Flavius Josephus, Hendrickson Publishers, Inc., 1987

The New Evidence That Demands a Verdict, Josh McDowell,Thomas Nelson Publishers, 1999

Epicenter, Joel Rosenberg, Tyndale House Publishers, Inc., 2006

Humanist Manifesto I and II, ed. Paul Kurtz, Prometheus Books, 1973

Memoir, G. Leibholz, in the preface before The Cost of Discipleship (by D. Bonhoeffer), Touchstone, 1995 (Previously published 1959)

Democracy in America, Alexis de Tocqueville, ed. Richard Heffner, Mentor Book, 1956

What Do Jews Believe, David S. Ariel, Shocken Books, New York,1995

The Apocalypse of Ahmadinejad, Mark Hitchcock, Multnomah books, 2007.

Abingdon Commentary for Twentieth Century Christians; "The Life of Jesus Christ" by Joseph McFadyen, p. 891; Frederick Carl Eiselen, ed. Doubleday and Co. 1929

Church of England website: www.cofe.anglican.org/info/statistics

The New Evidence That Demands a Verdict, Josh McDowell, Thomas Nelson Publishers, 1999

www.wycliffe.org

Innocents Abroad, Mark Twain. 1869

Systematic Theology, Wayne Grudem, Zondervan Publishing House, 1994

Answering Jewish Objections to Jesus, Vol. 1, Michael L. Brown, Baker Books, 2000

A Woman Rides the Beast, Dave Hunt, Harvest House Publishers, 1994

Coming: The End! Thomas McCall and Zola Levitt, Zola Levitt Ministries, 1999

The Seven Feasts of Israel, Zola Levitt, 1979; Zola Levitt Ministries, Dallas, Texas

Left Behind (Series), Tim LaHaye and Jerry Jenkins, 1995-2004, Tyndale House Publishers

The Last Battle, C.S. Lewis, HarperTrophy, 1956, pp. 194-195

Heaven, Randy Alcorn, Tyndale House Publishers, 2004;

Our Hands Are Stained With Blood, Michael L. Brown; Destiny Image Publishers, Inc., 1992

William Hayden Childs, MD, MBA

Dr. Childs is a physician and Bible teacher.  He has studied
prophetic Scriptures in the Bible for over 15 years.  In addition
to Medicine, he has read extensively in the areas of history
(especially Jewish and Christian), philosophy, and other world
religions.  He lives with his wife, Jule, on a farm in southeast
Alabama.